The BASIC Idea

AN INTRODUCTION TO COMPUTER PROGRAMMING

RICHARD FORSYTH

Software Manager of RAIR Timesharing, formerly with City of London Polytechnic Computer Service

LONDON

CHAPMAN AND HALL

A Halsted Press Book

John Wiley & Sons, New York

First published 1978
by Chapman and Hall Ltd,
11 New Fetter Lane, London EC4P 4EE
Reprinted 1978

Typeset by Hope Services, Wantage
and printed in Great Britain
by Richard Clay (The Chaucer Press) Ltd, Bungay, Suffolk

ISBN 0 412 21470 9

Distributed in the U.S.A. by Halsted Press.
A Division of John Wiley & Sons, Inc., New York

Library of Congress Cataloging in Publication Data

Forsyth, Richard
The basic idea
1. Basic (Computer program language)
I. Title
QA76.73B3F67 001.6'414 77-18533
ISBN 0-470-99397-9

Contents

Preface

The aim of this book is to provide a simple introduction to the Basic computer programming language. The spread of time-sharing systems - and, lately, of micro-processors - has brought computer power within reach of more and more people, many of whom would not, until recently, have even considered using a computer; and for a number of reasons Basic is one of the best means of employing this new-found power. Its down-to-earth structure makes it particularly suited to the first-time user.

Basic, although it has its faults, possesses three very important strong points: (1) it is easy to learn enough of the language to start using it for worth-while tasks in a very short time; (2) it offers powerful additional facilities for the more advanced user; and (3) it is designed for interactive use rather than batch-work. These advantages make it especially suitable for the non-professional. It is not surprising, therefore, that Basic is growing in popularity.

Moreover, for the future, we can see that the time is not far off when a complete desk-top computer with adequate main memory and a large backing store will cost about the same as a colour TV; and the overwhelming probability is that these personal computers of five or ten years hence will be programmed in Basic. So Basic could well become even more popular.

The interactive nature of Basic deserves emphasis, in contrast to the alternative method of 'batching'. Although there are batch-mode versions of Basic, and although many other programming languages have been adapted to run interactively (and some, like APL and POP-2, have also been designed that way), one of the chief distinctive features of Basic is that it was devised specifically for conversational use, where the user interacts with the computer system. This means that the programmer need not specify every contingency in advance, and can correct mistakes, or otherwise react to unforseen situations, as they arise. Anyone who is accustomed to a purely batch-work system, where one trivial error can abort a run and delay the final results by a day or more, will appreciate that this saves a great deal of frustration. The interactive approach is also extremely important to the new user. It allows the learner to experiment with the system. This, of course, can dramatically speed up the learning process; and a motto throughout this book will be 'when in doubt, try it out'. If you are not sure how something works, or whether it is allowed, make up a small test program and see what happens. This can be done quite quickly on-line; and the computer will very soon tell you if it is not permitted. To sum up, then, Basic lends itself to learning by hands-on practical experience.

These characteristics make Basic a very efficient medium of man-machine communication. There are many computing tasks for which the use of a Basic system is quite simply the easiest, quickest and most economical way to get the job done - and this becomes more true as computer time gets cheaper while human time gets more expensive.

Since Basic is less well standardized than some other computer languages, a decision had to be taken on what version to describe. The policy adopted in this book was to stick to one representative implementation of Basic. This means that all the demonstration programs and solutions to exercises have actually run on a particular machine - namely, a DEC System-10. (This machine is common in educational environments. Furthermore, its Basic is closer to the original Dartmouth Basic philosophy than many other extended Basic systems.) However, it does mean that some of the example programs will not run on other machines without modification. In most cases the modifications required will be slight. The essentials of the language, as described in Chapters 1 - 4, are virtually universal and common to all implementations; but many of the advanced features (Chapters 5 - 8) are not standard and the user may find differences on another computer. The major points of variation are covered more fully in the relevant sections. Once again, the way to find out how something works on your computer is to try it and see. The reader who has learned the language as described here should have little difficulty adapting to any version of Basic.

My thanks go to the City of London Polytechnic Computer Centre for use of their DEC System-10 computer on which all the example programs in this book were run. I would also like to thank Steve Rose, Mary White, my wife, my daughter and two bottles of imported wine for helping to devise the title of this book.

March 1977 Richard Forsyth

1. Getting started

Basic (an acronym for Beginner's All-purpose Symbolic Instruction Code) is a computer programming language devised in 1964 by Professors Kemeny and Kurtz of Dartmouth College, New Hampshire, U.S.A. Since then it has been developed by various manufacturers and institutions, and has to some extent diverged. Consequently several variants or 'dialects' now exist. The version described here is that used on the DEC System-10. The American National Standards Institute will shortly publish a specification for standard Basic, and although this will probably have some extra features not present in DEC Basic, it is most unlikely that it will lack any of the facilities described here, so there should be no conflict. In other words, standard Basic will be an extension of the language described in this guide.

The great attraction of Basic is that it is easy to learn. A novice should be able to write and execute a simple program in Basic after only one afternoon spent interacting with the Basic system on a terminal. The interactive nature of Basic is very important, and is one reason why it is easy to learn: it was specifically designed for interactive use, and is best learnt by interactive practice.

1.1 Timesharing

Fig. 1 sketches roughly the relationships among the main components of a fairly typical medium-sized educational computer system.

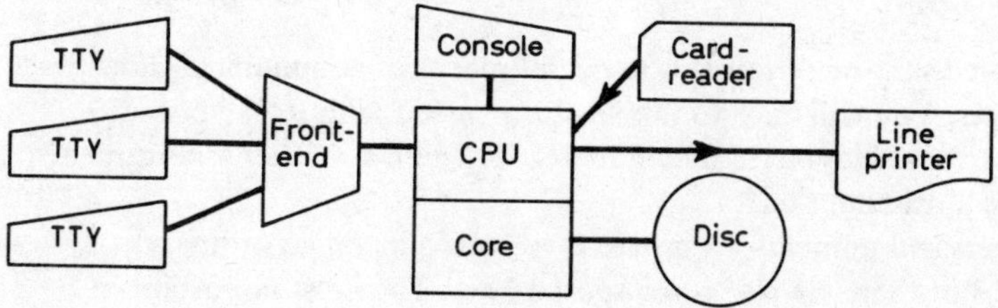

Fig. 1. Diagram of an educational timesharing system (DEC10).

The elements of this configuration are as follows: each TTY represents a terminal through which a user communicates with the system; the *front-end* is a minicomputer which handles communications between the terminals and the main processor; the CPU is the Central Processing Unit where calculations are actually performed, so closely related to the high-speed *core* store where programs and data reside while being processed that they are shown in the figure as two parts of the same thing; the *disc* is a magnetic backing-store device for long-term storage of programs and data; the *cardreader* and *lineprinter* are peripherals for the input and output of relatively large quantities of information; and the *console* is the operator's control console.

Fig. 1.1 should not be taken as an exact map of the installation but as a rough guide to its main components and their connections. In particular, the number of terminals shown is three; but the number actually connected to the system at any one time may vary from none to about 60.

One computer can serve many terminals simultaneously using a method known as timesharing. Essentially this involves sharing the main processor's time among several different tasks. Because the processor is so fast an individual user rarely notices any interruption, unless the system is very heavily loaded, although the computer will, in general, only devote a small fraction of its time - typically 1/50 of a second every second - to any one terminal. For the rest of the time that job is suspended: the program, its data and information about where it was suspended are held on backing-store so that it can be re-started at the right place when its turn for active processing comes round again.

Timesharing on the DEC10 is controlled by a set of supervisory programs collectively known as Monitor, with which the user interacts by issuing Monitor commands. Monitor controls the sharing of resources among jobs, and is active whenever the computer is running. It is the operating-system of the DEC10.

1.2 The keyboard

For the basic user, the terminal is the chief means of communication with the computer. You will have to familiarize yourself with its keyboard. A typical keyboard layout is shown in Fig. 2. There are other arrangements, but this the most common.

The letters and numbers are where they would be on an ordinary typewriter; but there are also some special keys. The most important of these are: Return which causes carriage-return and is used to terminate an

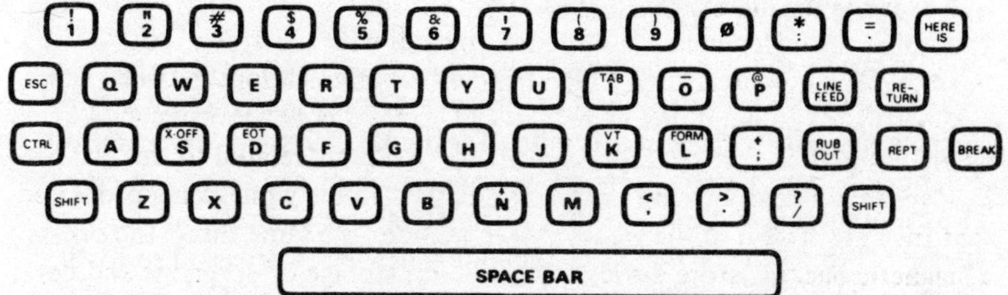

Fig. 2. Typical keyboard layout.

input line; Rub-out which erases the last character typed in; and CTRL which is used to produce the 'control' characters. The control characters have special effects and are obtained by holding down the CTRL key while typing the character concerned. For instance, control-C, which is represented in this text as CTRL/C and which causes a circumflex C to be printed (ˆC), is obtained by typing C while pressing CTRL at the same time.

CTRL/C halts a running Basic program when it is waiting for input; CTRL/O suppresses whatever is being printed by the computer; CTRL/U deletes an entire line of input; and so on. These special characters can be used from within the Basic system. They are more fully described in Appendix C.

It is essential for the beginner to get used to the keyboard, and the main requirement for this is practice. There is no need to be a star typist, but on the other hand if it takes you several seconds to hunt for every character then you will not find your terminal sessions very enjoyable, or productive.

Notice particularly that the number 1 is different from the letter I and that the number 0 is different from the letter O. The computer is very fussy about these distinctions: if you type one when you mean the other, it will cause problems. Unfortunately, not all keyboards mark the difference, except by position, so take note of where they are placed. You are advised to adopt the following handwriting conventions when preparing your own programs: it could save you quite a lot of trouble later when typing them into the computer.

Number	Letter
Ø	O
1	I
2	Z

1.3 Getting on and off the system

To gain access to the computer you will almost certainly have to go through some sort of identification procedure, known as 'logging in' or 'logging on'. The logging in procedure for the DEC System-10 is briefly described below. There is a family resemblance between logging in on most timesharing systems but they differ at various points: you are advised to find out the details of account codes, passwords and so forth, on the machine you will be using before going on. You will have to obtain a user-number or user-name if you do not already have one.

Logging in can be a chore for the newcomer, especially one who is not a good typist; but it is essential in order to do useful work on the computer.

1.3.1 Logging in (on the DEC10)

Ensure that your terminal is properly connected to the computer: switch it on and check the line.

Type LOGIN (one word, not two) when the computer signals its readiness by printing a full stop (period) at the left margin. Then press Return.

Reply to the number sign (#) with your PPN, which on the DEC10 is two numbers separated by a comma that identify you to the system e.g. 17022,1.

When it types PASSWORD: give your chosen password. This is one to six characters needed to convince the computer you are authorized to use that PPN. For security, it is not echoed on the terminal.

You should now get an introductory message stating the date, day and time, followed by a fullstop at the start of a new line. If you do not, type CTRL/C to abort the login and start again from scratch. If you do, type BASIC then Return to enter the Basic system. It should reply READY. You can now use the Basic system.

1.3.2 Logging out

Almost all Basic systems respond to the BYE command by disconnecting the user from the system in an orderly fashion. On some machines however (not the DEC10) BYE only causes exit from the Basic subsystem and another command is needed to leave it altogether. In either case it is vital not to forget to log out.

By just walking away leaving the terminal on-line you waste time and money, and you give the next stranger who uses that terminal the opportunity to erase or otherwise corrupt your stored programs and files - a temptation few people can entirely resist.

A complete terminal session, from login to logout, can be seen in Section 1.5.

1.4 The Basic system

We have already begun talking about a Basic system as well as the Basic language. Before attempting to write and run your own Basic programs, you must learn something about the workings of this system.

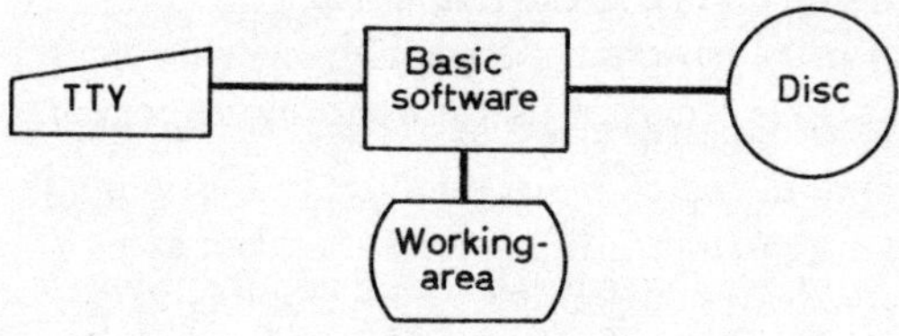

Fig. 3. Illustration of the Basic system.

The DEC10 Basic system as it appears to the user is outlined in Fig. 3. The average user will not need a more detailed picture than this. However, it is worth knowing that when you type in and run and save Basic programs you are not interacting directly with the computer but with some quite sophisticated software. For instance, the computer cannot obey the list of statements which constitute a Basic program unless they are first translated into machine instructions. A program to do this is one part of the Basic software, which can be divided into three major subsystems: a command decoder that accepts and carries out commands to run a program, to save a program on disc, to retrieve a program from disc, and so forth; a line-editor that enables you to delete or amend lines of the program in the working area; and an interpreter that translates programs from Basic into a form the machine can understand. By giving Monitor the command BASIC, you call up this system.

The major parts of the system depicted above are the user sitting at a terminal (TTY), the Basic software with which the user interacts in order to move programs between disc and working area or to run programs or to edit them, the disc where programs and data can be stored for later use, and the working area. It is important to be clear about the distinction between the working area where programs can be run and/or edited and the disc where they can be saved. Before you can execute or amend a program you must put it into the working area either by typing it in or by recalling it from disc if it is stored there. The usefulness of the disc store is that it allows you to save a program between sessions so that once your program is working satisfactorily you can keep it for later use without having to type it in afresh each time.

1.4.1 Using the Basic system

When using the Basic system you can be in one of two phases.

(1) Input - when Basic is accepting lines into the working area and obeying commands.

(2) Execution - when Basic is interpreting and obeying the program currently in the working area.

During the input phase (1) Basic regards any line starting with a number as a line to be added, at the point indicated by its number, to the contents of the working area. Any line not starting with a number is taken as a command. If Basic cannot recognize a command it simply complains (? WHAT?) so no damage is done by accidentally typing a nonsense command; but if you type a linenumber followed by garbage, that line will be faithfully added at the appropriate point to the contents of the working area and will not cause an error until you try executing it. (Some Basic systems translate each statement when it is typed in, but the DEC10 waits till you try to execute a program before checking for syntactic errors.)

During the execution phase (2) Basic tries to obey the program currently in the working area.

To get from phase (1) to phase (2), type the RUN command. To force exit from phase (2) and return to phase (1), type two CTRL/C's which should make Basic print READY. Normally Basic returns to phase (1) after reaching the end of the program.

Note that 'statements' (or 'instructions') are numbered lines making up the Basic program which can be executed by RUN; while 'commands' are the unnumbered lines, obeyed immediately, which tell Basic what to do next.

You can enter a Basic program by typing in the numbered statements to the Basic system in any order that suits you - thus building it up line-by-line in the working area. Alternatively, it can be recalled from disc with the OLD command if it is already stored there. Once in the working area, a program can be run by giving the RUN command.

1.4.2 Some Basic commands

Appendix C contains a full list of Basic commands. A much shorter list of the essential ones you will need to begin with is given below. Three-letter abbreviations, which are acceptable, are shown here: the full forms appear in Appendix C.

Command	Meaning
BYE	Leave the system.
CAT	List user's entries on disc store.
LIS	List current contents of working area
NEW spec	Clear contents of working area for input of new program, with specified name.
OLD spec	Retrieve the stored program specified and put it into working-area.
RUN	Execute the program currently in the working-area.
SAV spec	Save the contents of the working-area on disc, under the name and extension specified.
UNS spec	Erase (unsave) specified entry from disc store.

In this list the 'spec' stands for a DEC10 specification of a program (or file) which follows the command after a space. Each program is known to the system by a name and an 'extension', separated by a dot (full stop). The extension can be from 0 to 3 characters. If you leave it out it will be assumed to be BAS by the Basic system. The name is from 1 to 6 letters or numbers, chosen by the user. A typical specification might be TEST1.BAS which could appear in the command

OLD TEST1.BAS

telling the system to find TEST1.BAS on the user's disc area and bring it into the working-area - overwriting anything currently there.

If you leave out the spec from a NEW or OLD command Basic will remind you to give it; but if you leave out the spec from a SAV or UNS command, Basic assumes the current name and extension of whatever is in the working-area. Always consider what effect it will have on the contents of the working-area, and on the disc store, before giving a command.

1.4.3 The Basic library

If you follow the CAT command with three asterisks (CAT***) you will set a catalogue of the public Basic library programs which are accessible to all users. This library of programs includes many to perform commonly required calculations, as well as several games and demonstrations, which can be helpful in getting used to the keyboard and the system. To obtain one of these, follow its spec with three stars (***) in the OLD command: for example OLD MASTER.CLP*** loads MASTER.CLP from the Basic library into your working-area ready to be run by RUN.

All timesharing systems will maintain some sort of library of useful Basic programs for public access, but the precise method of getting one of them, as well as the content of the library, will vary from installation to installation.

1.5 Sample terminal session

Below is the printout from a complete terminal session, to show you examples of valid login and logout, and to give you an idea of what a Basic program looks like. Do not worry if you cannot yet understand how it works: the statements it uses are explained in the next Chapter. For the moment, all you need to notice is that a Basic program consists of a series of statements each preceded by a linenumber.

In this example, as in those which follow throughout this book, parts typed by the user have been printed in bold type to distinguish them from the computer's output. Anything not in bold type was printed by the computer.

```
.LOGIN
JOB 9 CITY POLY MONITOR 507B10 TTY146
#311/1
PASSWORD:
1730              12-MAR-76         FRI

.BASIC

READY, FOR HELP TYPE HELP.
OLD DEGREE.XXX

READY
LIS

DEGREE.XXX    17:31              12-MAR-76

10 REM* CENTIGRADE/FAHRENHEIT CONVERTER:
20 REM  F = 9/5*C+32
30 REM  C = (F–32)*5/9
40 PRINT "WHEN THE COMPUTER TYPES ? GIVE DEGREES, SCALE"
50 PRINT "SCALE SHOULD BE 1 (C) OR 2 (F)"
60 PRINT
100 INPUT D,S
110 IF S=1 THEN 200
120 IF S=2 THEN 300
```

```
130 PRINT "2ND NUMBER MUST BE 1(C->F) OR 2(F->C)"
140 PRINT "PLEASE TRY AGAIN"
150 GOTO 100
200 REM* CENTIGRADE TO FAHRENHEIT:
210 LET C=D
220 LET F=9/5*C+32
230 GOTO 400
300 REM* FAHRENHEIT TO CENTIGRADE:
310 LET F=D
320 LET C=(F-32)*5/9
400 PRINT C "CELSIUS IS "F" FAHRENHEIT"
410 IF C<-273 THEN 430
420 GOTO 100
430 PRINT "WHICH IS BELOW ABSOLUTE ZERO!"
440 REM* STOP HERE (TOO COLD)
999 END

READY
RUN

DEGREE.XXX    17:32              12-MAR-76

WHEN THE COMPUTER TYPES ? GIVE DEGREES,SCALE
SCALE SHOULD BE 1 (C) OR 2 (F)

?0,1
0  CELSIUS IS 32 FAHRENHEIT
?37,1
37  CELSIUS IS 98.6 FAHRENHEIT
?0, 2
-17.7778 CELSIUS IS 0 FAHRENHEIT
?100,1
100  CELSIUS IS 212 FAHRENHEIT
?100,2
37.7778  CELSIUS IS 100 FAHRENHEIT
?-4,0
2ND NUMBER MUST BE 1(C->F) OR 2(F->C)
PLEASE TRY AGAIN
?-40,2
-40  CELSIUS IS -40 FAHRENHEIT
?32,2
0  CELSIUS IS 32 FAHRENHEIT
```

```
?20,1
20 CELSIUS IS 68 FAHRENHEIT
?−460,2
−273.333 CELSIUS IS −460 FAHRENHEIT
WHICH IS BELOW ABSOLUTE ZERO!

TIME:            0.38 SECS

READY
BYE
JOB 9, USER [311,1] LOGGED OFF TTY146    1735    12-MAR-76
SAVED ALL FILES (197 BLOCKS)
RUNTIME 1.34 SEC
```

In this simple session the user logs in under the PPN 311,1 and then enters the Basic system. The program called DEGREE.XXX is retrieved from disc storage and loaded into the working-area by the OLD command. This program converts temperatures from centigrade to fahrenheit, or vice versa. It requires the user to give it two numbers - a temperature, and a number indicating the scale on which that temperature is measured - and then it prints out the temperature in both scales. If the temperature is below absolute zero the program halts after converting it, otherwise it asks for more input. The program is first listed by LIS and then run by RUN. Finally the user leaves the system by typing BYE.

1.6 The next step

It is time to get your hands on a terminal. The fastest way to learn to use the Basic system is by practice. Because of its interactive design, the system itself acts somewhat like a teaching machine. But before rushing wildly to the nearest keyboard, read this section, which discusses some common problems encountered by beginners.

1.6.1 Practical details

Certain skills which appear to have nothing to do with programming must be mastered in order to utilize the computer. Before going any further you should be reasonably confident that you know how to do the following things.

(1) Establish contact with the system: this may involve dialling up over the telephone network, and testing the line and/or terminal for malfunction.

(2) Gain access to the system: this will probably involve applying for (or buying) a user-number, account-code, PPN or whatever it is called.

It will also involve typing this id-code and password correctly and in the right format and order. Here you will first notice how finicky computers can be about apparently petty details like commas, spaces, new lines and so on.

(3) Get into the Basic system. This may or may not happen automatically when you log in - on the larger systems with a choice of languages it usually does not.

(4) Leave Basic and log out properly.

(5) Call in a stored (library) program.

(6) Execute a program in the working-area.

(7) List a program.

(8) Save a program for use at a later date.

(9) Delete a program from long-term storage.

(10) Halt a running program when something goes wrong.

(11) Erase one or more characters on the line you are currently typing, or erase the whole line, before transmitting it to the computer.

(12) Recognize the most common error messages and the states they signify.

You are strongly recommended to write down short notes (plus examples) of all these operations on a sheet of paper or postcard, and carry them around with you for the first couple of weeks - until they become ingrained. This card should also have your user-code on it (but keep your password in your head).

These necessary but arbitrary points are those which tend to cause most confusion and annoyance among people who have never used a computer before. The difficulties of learning Basic are minor by comparison.

It is important to get the feel of conversational computing; to get to know the keyboard and the effects of the various special keys; to master the essential procedures such as login and logout; and to gain a sense of competence in using the computer, before going on to your own programming projects. If the system is strange to you when you come to type in, edit and execute your own programs, you will experience needless frustration. A good way to practise these basic skills is to try running one of the public library programs.

1.6.2 Program design

Computers can be used, and misused. Two pitfalls to avoid when you start interacting with the computer are: firstly, sitting down at a terminal with no idea of what you plan to do; and secondly, attempting something too complex too soon and becoming discouraged. On the one hand your mind should not be blank when you first confront a terminal, and on the other hand you should not attempt anything overambitious (and fail) on your first session.

Remember also that programming is a problem-solving exercise, not purely a matter of coding. Once your problem is analysed, coding its solution should be relatively easy; but if you fail to understand it, or do not know exactly what you want the computer to do, the coding will be arduous and prone to error.

There are certain principles of good program design. The theme of well-structured programs will be taken up again at greater length in Chapter 8. Here it suffices to say that many beginners ignore these principles, as do many experienced programmers, largely because they are over-eager to get their programs running, and consequently spend too little time analysing the problem that the program is supposed to solve. Time spent in careful thought beforehand is usually handsomely repaid in time saved later trying to correct mistakes that stem from poor program design.

Each programmer develops an individual style; but it is as well to resolve at the outset to be as methodical as possible, and not to neglect the importance of thorough preliminary analysis.

2. Basic Basic

In order to make the computer do calculations for you, it is necessary to specify exactly the sequence of operations it must perform. In other words it must be given a 'program' (a list of instructions) in a language it can understand. One such language is Basic. A program in Basic consists of an ordered set of 'statements' each one of which instructs the computer to carry out single step in the computation. These statements are English keywords such as LET and PRINT sometimes followed by mathematical expressions or other symbols and always preceded by a linenumber.

Thus, to apply the computer to your particular problem, using Basic, you must first break the problem down into a detailed sequence of small steps, then write the Basic statements necessary to do those steps in the correct order. This will be a Basic program for that task, which you can type into the system and test-run, amending it where it does not work, until you have a successfully running version that can be saved on disc for subsequent re-use. This process is illustrated in Fig. 4.

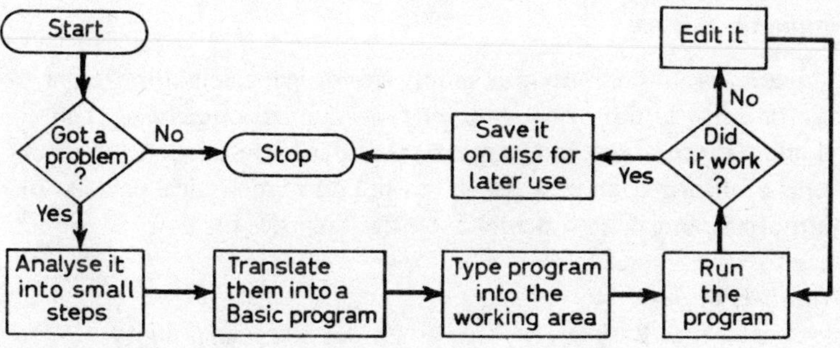

Fig. 4. The programming process, in Basic.

This is inevitably a simplified outline, but it does capture two important points: firstly, that the art (or science or business) of programming is a process, comprising several more or less well-defined stages; and secondly, that this process is essentially cyclic. The cyclic nature of the programming process is a key feature: once the program is in the working-area, the programmer repeatedly tests it then revises it, tests it then revises it . . . until it works satisfactorily and can be saved on disc.

Notice also that this diagram takes the form of a flowchart. Often a flowchart is useful in the initial stage - clarifying the problem. Very briefly, a flowchart exhibits the main steps of a process, distinguishing decisions (diamond-shaped boxes) from activities or operations (rectangular boxes) and linking these by arrows indicating the order in which they are performed. A flowchart is often a good way both to help analyse a problem at the beginning and to present the logic of its solution at the end. Flowcharting has its own standards and conventions which are not dealt with further here, but the beginner will still find that simple flowcharts using only decisions and operations can be very useful.

This chapter introduces seven essential Basic statements. They form a foundation of the language on which you can build as you progress. There are many programming tasks which cannot be carried out easily, or at all, using only these seven statements; but, equally, there is also a surprisingly wide variety of tasks which can be. Moreover, it would be hard to find a Basic program of any size which did not use most, or all, of them. So you will find it hard to write Basic programs without knowing all these statements, and you will find it possible to write many interesting programs using only them. (Incidentally, the example program DEGREE.XXX in Section 1.5 employs all these seven statement types, and no others.)

2.1 Arithmetic in Basic

Many people think of computers as simply overgrown calculators - large machines for doing nothing but arithmetic, or 'number-crunchers'. You will find later (for instance, in Chapter 6) that Basic can be used for other kinds of information processing, but of course numerical calculation is very important and Basic provides extensive facilities for it.

2.1.1 Numbers in Basic

Numeric constants in Basic are written as a series of decimal digits optionally preceded by a sign and optionally containing a decimal point. They may also be followed by an exponent part - the letter E followed by an optional sign followed by one or two digits. Leading zeroes are not significant. Examples of valid numeric constants in Basic are shown below.

Integral: 0,1,−999,+1,12345678,002,200
Fixed-point: 0.7,1.6,−89.305,1000.0001,72.0,−9.87654321
Floating-point: 1E7,0.314159265E01,4E+2,5E−11,−99.99E9.

Commas are not allowed within a number, so twelve thousand is 12000 and not 12,000. The commas above were inserted merely as separators between numbers. In floating-point notation the E stands for 'times ten to the power of', and is used for scaling. Thus 1E7 equals one times ten to the power of seven which is ten million (10000000), and 0.314159265E01 is an approximation to pi (3.14159265). This is sometimes called 'scientific notation'.

Internally numbers are stored in two parts, a fractional part and an exponent part, but this need not concern the novice. The largest possible positive number in DEC10 Basic is about 1.7E38 (or 17 followed by 37 zeroes) and the smallest is approximately 1.4E-39. Larger or smaller values cause 'overflow' or 'underflow' respectively. When overflow occurs a warning is printed and the computation proceeds using the largest number the computer can hold (1.7E38); when underflow occurs a message is printed and the computation proceeds using zero. Negative numbers are limited to the same range, with opposite sign.

There is little point in writing more than eight significant figures in a constant, although it is legal, since the computer's calculations are restricted to eight digits of precision. (It is possible to write Basic programs that overcome the limitations on size and accuracy mentioned here, but this requires extra programming effort.)

2.1.2 Variables

A number represents a fixed value in a program. It is a constant. A value that can alter during program execution is known as a variable.

In Basic, variables are given names which can be a single letter or a letter followed by one digit. Thus A1,B,X,Z9 could all be variable-names but 1A,QB,X50,Z99 could not. The name of a variable is chosen by the programmer (usually with some mnemonic association) to refer to a variable quantity. You can think of variables as storage locations for holding one number, which may change during the course of the computation. A variable's name is used in the program to represent the number currently held in that location. (It is also used in a different context to change the contents of that location.)

Note: In DEC10 Basic, although not in all versions of Basic, numeric variables are pre-set to zero at the start of a program's run. It is unwise, however, to depend on this feature: better practice is to initialize all variables yourself, even if they start as zero.

2.1.3 Arithmetic expressions

Arithmetic expressions in Basic follow normal algebraic conventions as closely as possible within the constraints that all symbols must lie on one line and that all operators must be explicit, not implied. An elementary arithmetic (or numeric) expression (or formula) takes one of the two forms

Item
Item Operator Item

where Item can be a constant or a variable-name, and where Operator is one of the arithmetic operators. More complex expressions can be built up by substituting a complete expression for an Item according to the pattern

Expression Operator Expression

where Expression is either of the two simple forms above, or itself a more complex expression. Expressions and subexpressions may be enclosed in brackets.

The arithmetic operators, in order of precedence, are:

^ or **	exponentiation;
* and /	multiplication and division;
+ and −	addition and subtraction.

The order of precedence is important. When evaluating an expression Basic follows these rules to produce the final result:

(1) Evaluate subexpressions in brackets, if any;
(2) Evaluate any exponentiations (left to right);
(3) Evaluate multiplications and divisions (left to right);
(4) Evaluate additions and subtractions (left to right).

Thus A+B*2 means first multiply B by 2 then add A; while (A+B)*2 means add A to B then multiply their sum by two. Notice that paired brackets may be used to impose any desired order of evaluation, if the default priorities are not suitable. The picture is somewhat complicated by the fact that the plus and minus signs can assume three distinct roles. The three roles of the minus sign, for instance, are as the sign of a number (−5), and the negation operator requiring only one operand (−B), and as the subtraction operator (5−B). Confusion can be avoided by judicious insertion of zeroes and brackets. The best policy for the beginner is to avoid very long complex expressions where possible, by breaking them down into simpler steps, and to insert brackets wherever ambiguity might arise - even if not strictly necessary.

A few examples will help clarify these rules. (Assume that A=1, B=2, C=10, X=−1, Z=0.)

Expression	Result
+1	1
X	−1
−A	−1
−X	1
A+10	11
A−B	−1
C*10	100
A/B	0.5
A/B+C	10.5
A/(B+C)	0.08333333
4*B^2	16
(4*B)^2	64
B*C/(4−X)+A	5

As a further illustration, consider what happens when the final example is evaluated.

B*C/(4−X)+A	Original expression
2*10/(4−(−1))+1	Substitute values of variables
2*10/(4+1)+1	Evaluate innermost parenthesis
2*10/5+1	Evaluate bracketted subexpression
20/5+1	Leftmost multiplication
4+1	Division
5	Addition

Incidentally, spaces are not significant in arithmetic expressions, so A + B− C means the same as A+B−C. To round off this section, here is a list of illegal expressions, with short explanations of why they are not valid. A very common mistake is not having the same number of left and right brackets in an expression.

Invalid expression	Reason
1+	Nothing after +
AB+1	Illegal variable name
A.B	Multiplication is * not .
7B/2	7B not variable or expression
X&Y\Z	& and \ not operators

Q//A	Double division operator
4E*5	No exponent after E
(A+B)/C)	Too many right-brackets
J^J–50E50	Constant too large
98.6.	Too many decimal points
123,456+I	Comma not allowed in a number
(Q5+B	Extra left bracket, not paired
*#!!?	Gibberish
AAAAARGHH!!!!!	OK, don't panic! We've finished

Lines 220 and 320 of the example in Section 1.5 contain valid expressions.

2.2 The LET statement

The LET statement assigns a new value to a variable. Its general form is

linenumber LET variable-name = expression

where the word LET is optional, where the variable-name is the name of a variable, and where the expression is a valid arithmetic expression. It causes the expression on the right of the equal sign to be evaluated and then assigns the resultant value to the variable named on the left. The LET statement, then, has two functions: firstly, to evaluate a formula; and secondly, to alter the value of a variable. LET statements appear on lines 210,220,310 and 320 of the sample program DEGREE.XXX in Section 1.5. Other examples follow.

```
50 LET A = 1
100 LET Q5=0
200 LET J=J+1
300 LET I=(I*(I–1)) / (A*I)
500 E9 = 1E9
885 LET A=B=C=1000
```

Line 50 sets the variable A to equal 1. Line 100 sets Q5 to zero. Line 200 increments J by one - first evaluating the expression J+1 then assigning this value to replace the old value of J. Line 300 also has a variable appearing on both sides of the equal-sign (I). Line 500 sets the variable E9 to 1E9 which is 1000000000 or one thousand million, and shows that the word LET can be dropped: any statement not beginning with a recognized keyword is assumed to be a LET statement. Line 885 sets A and B and C to equal 1000. This last example is another extension of the LET statement, in which several variables are given the same value.

2.3 Six Basic statements

Six further Basic statements are now described which, together with LET, form the core of the Basic language. With them you can start to write useful Basic programs.

END

We start, deliberately, at the end. Every Basic program must have one (and only one) END statement. It must be the last line in the program: that is, it must have the highest linenumber. Its format is

linenumber END

and its purpose is to indicate the end of the program to the Basic interpreter. When the END is reached execution halts, Basic prints the runtime used by the program and READY, and the system reverts to its input phase awaiting user commands or additions to the working-area (see Section 1.4.1).

END is used on line 999 of the example program in Section 1.6.

GOTO

Unless specifically diverted, program execution is in ascending linenumber order. GOTO interrupts normal flow of processing and causes transfer to a specified line. Its form is

linenumber GOTO linenumber

and its effect is to cause the statement on the line with the second linenumber to be the next one executed, instead of the line immediately after the GOTO itself. Its purpose is to allow branching to another part of the program. Thus in the program

```
100 REM*APPROACHING A GOTO:
110 GOTO 200
120 REM*THIS LINE IS SKIPPED*
200 END
```

line 120 is never reached because line 110 instructs the computer to take the next instruction from line 200 (which stops the program).

This statement is used on lines 150,230 and 420 of the example program in Section 1.5.

IF

This statement diverts normal sequential flow of processing only if a given relationship holds. It permits conditional transfer to another part of the program, depending on the current state of program variables. The IF statement introduces the possibility of 'decision-making' into Basic. It is essential to any non-trivial program. Its form is

linenumber IF formula relation formula THEN linenumber

where the formulas are arithmetic expressions, as described in Section 2.1 and the relation is one of the following.

<	less than
>	greater than
=	equal to
<=	less than or equal to
>=	greater than or equal to
<>	not equal to

It causes a jump to the statement with the specified line-number if the relation holds between the two formulas; otherwise the statement immediately after the IF is the next one executed. Two examples follow.

```
100 IF A<10 THEN 50
200 IF A*B^2 >= 2E8 THEN 999
```

In the first (line 100) the computer is told to go back to line 50 if the value of A is less than 10, and otherwise to carry on with the statement following line 100. In the second (line 200) the computer is told to multiply A by B squared and compare the result with 2E8 (200 000 000). If it is greater than or equal to 2E8 then the next statement executed will be that on line 999, otherwise it will be the statement following line 200.

Thus the programmer can test whether conditions have occurred during processing and make the program do different things depending on the result of the test. Without this facility of selection, meaningful programming would be almost impossible.

Examples of IF statements can be found on lines 110,120 and 410 of the example program in Section 1.5.

INPUT

This statement calls for values from the user's terminal. It is a way to get data from the user into the program during execution. Its form is

linenumber INPUT list

where the list is a series of one or more variable-names (not expressions) separated by commas. When executed it causes the computer to print a question-mark, and wait for user input. The program will only continue when the user has supplied values for all variables in the list. Thus

```
500 INPUT A, B, X1
```

causes ? to appear on the user's terminal. The computer pauses, expecting the user to type precisely three numbers, separated by commas and terminated by Return, which will become the new values for A,B and X1 respectively. If you type fewer numbers than there are variables in the input list, it will repeat the ? and wait for more input; if you type too many numbers it will warn you that the extra ones have been ignored, and carry on. Take care to type as many numbers as there are variables on the input list: strange side-effects can arise from mistakes like typing 3,4,5 instead of 3,4.5 and similar small slips.

INPUT allows the user to interact with a running Basic program by giving new values to its variables. It can be seen in use on line 100 of the example program DEGREE.XXX in Section 1.5.

PRINT

This is used for output to the terminal. Its form is

linenumber PRINT list

where the list is a list of expressions, separated by commas or semicolons. The values of the expressions are calculated, and printed in order on the terminal. A carriage-return and line-feed are performed at the end of each PRINT statement, unless the list of expressions ends with a comma or semicolon. Two examples follow.

```
45 PRINT 10,A,10/A
90 PRINT "VALUE NUMBER";J;"IS";A/(A-1)*J
```

The first one would cause the line

```
10              20              0.5
```

to be printed (assuming A=20); and the second would cause

```
VALUE NUMBER 2 IS 2.10526
```

to be printed (assuming J=2). Note that items in the PRINT list separated by semicolons are printed closely packed with only a space between them while items separated by commas are spaced out, 5 per 72-character terminal line.

Some additional points worth noting concerning PRINT are:

(1) A PRINT statement with no output list causes one blank line to be printed;

(2) Ending an output list with a comma or semicolon suppresses the new line normally output at the end of each PRINT, so that the next PRINT will add more output starting where the last one finished;

(3) String constants (sequences of characters enclosed in double-quotes) may be items in an output list, as in line 90 above, in which case they are printed just as they appear, without the quotes.

Further information on PRINT can be found in Chapter 4. It is shown in use on lines 40,50,60,130,140,400 and 430 of the example in Section 1.5.

REM

This statement is often regarded as unimportant by the new programmer, and by many experienced programmers; although some experts believe that not less than half the lines in every program should be REM statements!

It is simply a means of putting remarks or comments in the body of a program. Its form is

linenumber REM text

where the text can be any printable characters. Its purpose is to allow the insertion of explanatory remarks in a program. Programs can be written without REM statements and can run successfully without them, but you will find they are useful when you come to revise a program written earlier by you - or, still worse, by someone else. Usually it only takes a couple of weeks to forget what the variables were for, why the program made certain tests rather than others, and indeed how on earth it worked at all. If you take the precaution of sprinkling your programs liberally with explanatory comments, these problems will be minimized.

Comments can also be added to any other statement (except an 'image' line or DATA statement, described in Chapter 4) after an apostrophe. Thus

```
660 LET G = P*453.6
```

has the same effect as

```
660 LET G = P*453.6 'CONVERT POUNDS(P) TO GRAMMES(G)
```

except that the latter has a remark added to explain what is going on. Do not, therefore, despise the humble REM statement: it can save you many headaches if used wisely.

If execution reaches a REM, nothing happens. It is ignored and control passes on to the next statement. Therefore it is quite permissible to have a statement such as GOTO 950 where line 950 is a REM statement.

REM can be seen on lines 10,20,30,200,300 and 440 of the sample program in Section 1.5.

2.4 Editing

As mentioned in Section 1.4, a Basic program is normally built up line-by-line in the working-area by typing lines in, preceded by appropriate linenumbers, via the terminal. Remember that lines can be entered in any order you like - being sorted automatically by the Basic system - and that every line in a Basic program must have its own unique linenumber, in the range from 0 to 99999. These numbers serve two purposes: they determine the order in which the statements are executed; and they identify lines for correction or insertion when the program is being edited.

It is very likely that when you first type in a program it will contain errors - misspellings, typing errors, mistakes in the syntax of the Basic language, and so forth. It is very easy to correct these in Basic, by replacing the lines which are wrong. Consider the effect of typing the following six lines.

```
10 REM*FIRST LINE
20 REM*2ND LINE
50 END
30 REM*THIRD LINE
20 REM*NEW SECOND LINE
40 REM*LINE 4
```

The result of typing these lines in this order is to leave the following 5 lines in the working-area, in the order shown.

```
10 REM*FIRST LINE
20 REM*NEW SECOND LINE
30 REM*THIRD LINE
40 REM*LINE 4
50 END
```

The lines have been sorted into ascending order, and the second version of line 20 has overwritten the first. If at this point we were to type a line numbered 35 it would be placed between lines 30 and 40.

In order to replace a line of the working-area that is incorrect, just type its linenumber then the line as it should be and end it with Return. The new line will overwrite the old one. To delete a line altogether, just type its linenumber followed immediately by Return, and that line will be erased from the working-area.

For deleting large groups of lines the command DELETE (or DEL) is available. DEL 90 deletes line 90; DEL 90-500 deletes lines 90 to 500 inclusive; DEL 90,500-600 deletes line 90 and lines 500 to 600 inclusive; and so on. The DEL command refers to the current contents of the working-area.

These editing techniques are sufficient for most cases, and are shown in action in Section 2.5.

Note: It is best to number the lines of a program in steps of five or ten to leave room for lines to be inserted in the middle when it is being revised.

2.5 Example session

The following example is the printout of a terminal session from entering the Basic system with BASIC to leaving it with BYE. In it a program called SIMPLE.XXX for adding a series of numbers input on the terminal is typed in, tested, and revised - demonstrating the cyclic character of the programming process and giving several illustrations of editing with the Basic line-editor.

Be warned that the first version of this program, typed after the NEW command, contains three mistakes. Firstly, INPUT is spelt INPUX on line 20; but this is immediately corrected by pressing Rubout to delete the X and then typing the T. Secondly, PRINT is mistyped as PTINT on line 70; and this is detected in the attempted RUN at 17:45. And thirdly, the END statement is omitted, which causes the second error-message. Both errors are rectified after the attempted run of 17:45 by typing lines 70 and 99 as they should have been. The corrected program is shown in the listing of 17:46.

```
.BASIC

READY, FOR HELP TYPE HELP.
NEW SIMPLE.XXX

READY
1 REM*ADDING AND AVERAGING PROGRAM:
10 LET T=N=0
20 INPUX\X\T X
```

```
30 IF X=-999 THEN 70
33 REM*-999 MEANS END OF DATA*
40 T=T+X        'ADD X TO TOTAL
50 N=N+1        'ADD 1 TO NUMBER
60 GOTO 20
70 PTINT N,T,T/N
RUN

SIMPLE.XXX    17:45          02-APR-76

? INITIAL PART OF STATEMENT NEITHER MATCHES A STATEMENT
KEYWORD NOR HAS A FORM LEGAL FOR AN IMPLIED LET -
CHECK FOR MISSPELLING IN LINE 70

? NO END INSTRUCTION

TIME: 0.06 SECS.

READY
99 END
70 PRINT N,T,T/N
LIS

SIMPLE.XXX    17:46          02-APR-76

1 REM*ADDING AND AVERAGING PROGRAM:
10 LET T=N=0
20 INPUT X
30 IF X=-999 THEN 70
33 REM* -999 MEANS END OF DATA*
40 T=T+X        'ADD X TO TOTAL
50 N=N+1        'ADD 1 TO NUMBER
60 GOTO 20
70 PRINT N,T,T/N
99 END

READY
RUN

SIMPLE.XXX    17:46          02-APR-76

?7
?77
?777
?7777
```

```
?77777
?777777
?7777777
?-999
7                  8641969            1234567

TIME: 0.12 SECS

READY
2  PRINT "HOW MANY NUMBERS TO BE ADDED";
3  INPUT N9
4  IF N9<=0 THEN 99                   'TOO FEW
5  IF N9>100 THEN 99                  'TOO MANY
15  REM*T=TOTAL,N=CASES:  BOTH SET TO NIL**
20  PRINT "VALUE";N+1;"IS";
30  INPUT X
33
60  IF N<N9 THEN 20                   'GET MORE INPUT
70  REM*PRINT RESULTS:
75  PRINT
80  PRINT "NUMBER", "TOTAL", "MEAN"
85  PRINT N,T,T/N
90  PRINT
95  GOTO 2       'GET NEXT GROUP
LIS

SIMPLE.XXX    17:51              02-APR-76

1  REM*ADDING AND AVERAGING PROGRAM:
2  PRINT "HOW MANY NUMBERS TO BE ADDED";
3  INPUT N9
4  IF N9<=0 THEN 99                   'TOO FEW
5  IF N9>100 THEN 99                  'TOO MANY
10  LET T=N=0
15  REM*T=TOTAL,N=CASES:  BOTH SET TO NIL*
20  PRINT "VALUE";N+1;"IS";
30  INPUT X
40  T=T+X        'ADD X TO TOTAL
50  N=N+1        'ADD 1 TO NUMBER
60  IF N<N9 THEN 20                   'GET MORE INPUT
70  REM*PRINT RESULTS:
75  PRINT
```

```
80 PRINT "NUMBER", "TOTAL", "MEAN"
85 PRINT N,T,T/N
90 PRINT
95 GOTO 2        'GET NEXT GROUP
99 END

READY
RUN

SIMPLE.XXX     17:52          02-APR-76

HOW MANY NUMBERS TO BE ADDED ?8
VALUE 1 IS ?0
VALUE 2 IS ?1
VALUE 3 IS ?2
VALUE 4 IS ?4
VALUE 5 IS ?8
VALUE 6 IS ?16
VALUE 7 IS ?32
VALUE 8 IS ?64

NUMBER         TOTAL          MEAN
8              127            15.875

HOW MANY NUMBERS TO BE ADDED ?5
VALUE 1 IS ?-999
VALUE 2 IS ?1001
VALUE 3 IS ?100
VALUE 4 IS ?99.99
VALUE 5 IS ?2001

NUMBER         TOTAL          MEAN
5              2202.99        440.598

HOW MANY NUMBERS TO BE ADDED ?0

TIME: 0.26 SECS.

READY
SAV

READY
CAT

DEGREE.XXX
SIMPLE.XXX
```

```
READY
BYE
```

The program is extensively edited during this session. The original version (listed at 17:46, run at 17:46) uses the number −999 as a 'sentinel' to signal that no further input is needed; the final version (listed at 17:51, run at 17:52) requires the user to specify how many numbers are to be added before they are input, and checks on line 60 whether it has received enough. Both methods are quite common. The sentinel method is useful if you do not know in advance how many values are to be input, but it means that one value (−999 in this case) cannot be read as data (and in the second run, at 17:52, −999 actually appears as input).

Compare the listings at 17:46 and at 17:51 to see what changes have been made by the lines typed in between (starting after the run of 17:46). Among other things, the printing of results has been made clearer by the addition of headings and blank lines. The later version can also handle more than one group of numbers in one run – deciding on lines 4 and 5 whether to stop or go on.

If after studying this example you still have doubts about how the program works or about how it is edited, try it out yourself.

2.6 Exercises

These exercises only ask you to write a program to perform a given task, but to do them fully you should write the program, type it in, and test-run it until it is working.

Sample solutions for all exercises marked by asterisks * are given at the end of the book.

(1) Write a program to print the first N numbers and their squares, where N is input by the user.

(2) Write a program to accept 2 numbers, A and B, and print: A+B, A−B, A*B, A/B, A^B.

(3) Write a program to convert an amount of francs into pounds sterling or vice versa using 1 pound = 9.09 francs (or the latest exchange rate). Later extend it to work either way.

*(4) Write a program to convert miles to kilometres OR yards to metres OR inches to centimetres OR vice versa (OR, later, both ways) using the fact that 0.9144 m = 1 yd and 2.54 cm = 1 in.

(5) Input a number and print it, its square, cube and reciprocal under appropriate headings.

(6) Input a radius (R) and print the area of that circle using 3.14159 as Pi and Pi*R^2 as the area of a circle, radius R.

(7) Input a number N and compute the factorial of N (N!) which is 1*2*3*4 . . . *(N–1)*N.

*(8) Write a program to compute compound interest, accepting a starting amount (A), an interest rate percentage (P), and a number of years (Y), and printing the final amount after Y years at P % interest.

(9) Write a program to accept N pairs of numbers which are distances in feet and inches and compute their total distance in inches, and in feet and inches.

(10) Write a program to accept N pairs of numbers representing times in hours and minutes and print their total in minutes, and in hours and minutes (later add seconds).

These exercises are roughly in increasing order of difficulty; but they can all be attempted using only the essential Basic statements:
LET, IF . . . THEN, GOTO, PRINT, INPUT, END, REM.

Note: Make sure you write down the program you plan to type in before sitting down at the terminal, and that you have a reasonably clear idea of what you are going to do: this saves valuable terminal time.

3. Loops and lists

3.0 Loops and lists

The computer really comes into its own when required to perform repetitive tasks. Very many computing processes take the form of a loop. In general, a loop may be flowcharted as in Fig. 5.

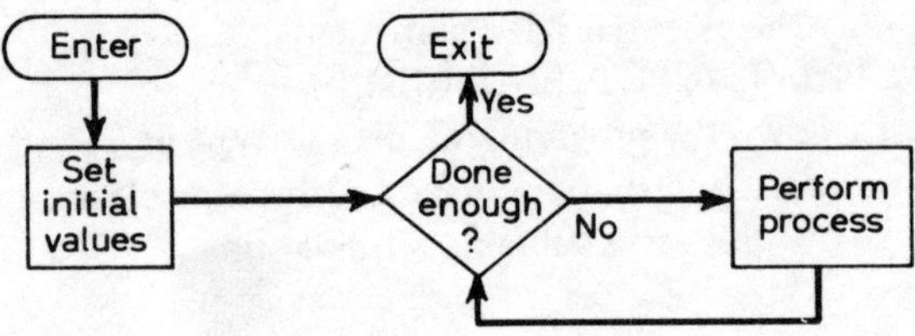

Fig. 5. Generalized loop.

A process whose flowchart takes this shape is called iterative. This general flowchart allows for the possibility that the process will not be executed even once - if the exit condition is satisfied at the start. One way such a process may be realized in Basic is by one or more IF statements then a block of statements to be repeated until the exit condition is satisfied and then a GOTO back to the beginning of the loop. The example SIMPLE.XXX in Section 2.5 was built round a loop. A listing and test-run of a simple iterative program follows.

```
LIST

LOOPY 2          16:07               31-MAR-76

10 REM* LOOP THE LOOP:
20 LET X=2       'INITIALIZE X
30 IF X>66000 THEN 99                'ENOUGH?
35 REM*GETS HERE IF X NOT TOO BIG*
40 PRINT X
50 X=X*2         'DOUBLE X
```

```
60  GOTO 30      'REPEAT PROCESS
99  END

READY
RUN

LOOPY2           16:07              31-MAR-76

2
4
8
16
32
64
128
256
512
1024
2048
4096
8192
16384
32768
65536

TIME: 0.08 SECS.

READY
```

This prints the first 16 powers of 2.

3.1 FOR and NEXT

Often a loop depends on a counter: the process is simply repeated a number of times. In order to simplify programming this kind of loop, Basic provides the FOR and NEXT statements. Below are two programs, both for printing the reciprocals of the first ten integers. One uses IF and GOTO statements; the other uses FOR and NEXT.

```
RECIP1
10 REM*LOOPING WITH IF AND GOTO:
20 PRINT "NUMBER", "RECIPROCAL"
30 LET X=1      'INITIALIZATION
40 IF X>10 THEN 99               'END OF LOOP?
```

```
50 PRINT X,1/X
60 LET X=X+1                'INCREMENT X
70 GOTO 40                  'BACK AGAIN
99 END
```

```
RECIP2
10 REM*LOOPING WITH FOR AND NEXT:
20 PRINT "NUMBER", "RECIPROCAL"
30 FOR X=1 TO 10                  'START OF LOOP
40    PRINT X, 1/X
50 NEXT X      'INCREMENT AND REPEAT IF UNFINISHED
99 END
```

Both produce the same results, but the second is more concise. The general form of the FOR statement is

linenumber FOR index = first-value TO last-value STEP increment

where the index can be any variable-name, first-value and last-value are arithmetic expressions giving the first and last value it will have, and the increment is another expression giving the amount to be added to the index-variable each time the loop is repeated. The word STEP may be replaced by BY and the entire STEP/BY part may be omitted (as in the example RECIP2) in which case an increment of +1 is assumed.

Each FOR statement must have a matching NEXT, using the same index-variable. Its form is

linenumber NEXT variable

where the variable is the same one used as the index in the FOR statement opening the loop. At the NEXT this variable is incremented and tested: if it is greater than the final value specified in the FOR execution passes on to the following statement, if not execution returns to the statement just after the FOR.

In the example RECIP2 line 30 opens the loop, line 40 is the process that is repeated 10 times, and line 50 closes the loop. Normally the central body of a loop is longer than one statement, but this is a very simple example.

The formula after STEP (or BY) may be negative. If it is, the variable is decremented and the loop repeated until it is less than the terminal value specified in the FOR - as opposed to greater than that value when the increment is positive.

It is possible to jump out of a loop with GOTO or IF, thus ending it prematurely, but it is illegal to jump into the middle of one. The only legal way into a FOR/NEXT loop is through the FOR statement. (On normal exit from a FOR loop via NEXT, the value of the index-variable is equal to the last-value given in the FOR statement. After abnormal exit, by jumping out, it is equal to the current value at the time of the jump.)

Loops may be nested, one inside the other, as exemplified in Section 3.3; but they may not overlap. The inner loop(s) must be completely enclosed within the outer one(s). The following examples should clarify this difference.

Valid nesting

```
10 FOR I=1 TO 20
20     FOR K=0 TO 20 BY 2
30         PRINT I*K
40     NEXT K
50 NEXT I
99 END
```

Invalid nesting

```
10 FOR I=1 TO 20
20 FOR K=0 TO 20 BY 2
30 PRINT I*K
40 NEXT I
50 NEXT K
99 END
```

In the invalid example on the right the program tries to end the (outer) loop involving I before the inner one using K, which is not allowed. Of two nested loops, the one which starts first must finish second.

FOR and NEXT are shown in use in the example in Section 3.3.

3.2 Arrays

It is frequently desirable to denote a group or collection of data by one name, and to distinguish individual members or elements by numbers. A set of data-items having one name is known as an 'array', and the number identifying a particular item in the set is called a 'subscript'. In Basic, an array is simply a collection of numbers (string arrays are covered in Chapter 6).

Arrays may have one or two 'dimensions'. A one-dimensional array is termed a 'vector', or sometimes a 'list'; a two-dimensional array is also called a 'matrix' or 'table'. (Three-dimensional arrays are permitted in some implementations of Basic, and arrays of four or more dimensions are permitted in some languages, such as Fortran; but we shall not be concerned with them here.)

A vector is essentially an ordered list of variable quantities. If an ordinary ('scalar') variable is thought of as a storage location for holding one number then a vector is a row of locations for holding several numbers. A ten-element vector (A) is depicted in Fig. 6.

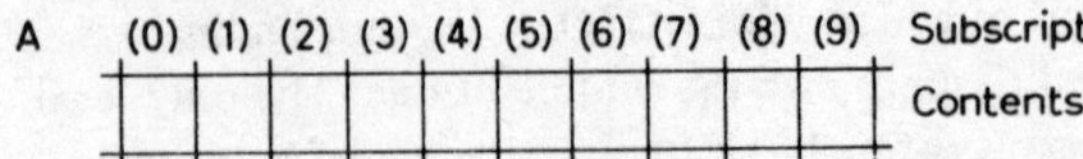

Fig. 6. Ten-element vector, named A.

An individual item in this vector is designated by following the array-name with a subscript expression in brackets. Thus A(1) refers to element 1 in A and A(9) to element 9, the last one; while A(I+J) refers to the I+Jth element (note that the lowest-numbered element is number zero).

A subscript may be a constant, variable or expression. If the subscript has a non-integer value it is truncated to the nearest lower value. Thus A(5.25) and A(5.75) both refer to the fifth element of A. If the subscript expression is out of bounds - below 0 or above the array's maximum - Basic reports an execution-error and halts the program.

A matrix is essentially a table of values. Matrices are usually described in terms of rows and columns. In order to identify an item in a matrix, two subscripts are required. A 15-element matrix (B) with 3 rows and 5 columns is illustrated in Fig. 7.

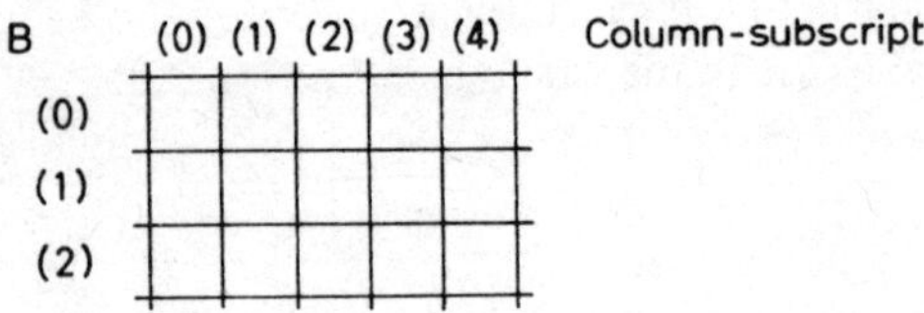

Fig. 7. Fifteen-element matrix, named B.

Each box in this diagram is capable of holding one number, and is designated by following the array-name with two subscripts in brackets separated by a comma. Conventionally the first is considered to identify the row and the second the column, so that B(0,2) refers to the cell on row 0, column 2 (not row 2 column 0). Again, the subscripts can be any arithmetic expressions and are truncated if not integral. Subscript values that are out of bounds cause error-messages.

Two statements using arrays are shown below.

```
700 LET A = K(I–1)*2
800 PRINT X(I,5)
```

In the first (line 700) A is set to double the value of element I—1 in the vector K. If I were 10 this would be element 9; if I were 9 this would be element 8; and so on. In the second example (line 800) the value of the element at row I, column 5 of the matrix X is printed.

Vectors and matrices give the programmer a means of organizing data. Many operations on sets of data, such as sorting a list of numbers into order which is considered in Section 3.3, would be virtually impossible without arrays.

3.2.1 The DIM statement

We have not so far said how arrays are set up. The DIM statement is used for this purpose. Its form is

linenumber DIM name(size), name(size) . . .

and its purpose is to declare the name and size of one or more arrays, and to reserve space for them. The size is one number (a constant, not a variable or expression) for vectors or two numbers separated by a comma in the case of matrices. The trailing dots indicate that several arrays may be dimensioned in the same DIM statement. Some examples follow.

```
25 DIM Q(5)
50 DIM A(20), B(7,8), Z1(200)
75 DIM I(99), J(3,20)
```

Like a variable-name, the name of an array may be either a letter or a letter and a digit. In fact it is possible to use the same name for a variable and an array (but not for a one-dimensional and a two-dimensional array) in one program - though this is seldom wise. DIM statements may appear anywhere in a program, although they are usually placed at or near the beginning. The numbers in brackets give the upper limits for the array subscripts: the minimum is always zero. Thus line 25 declares a one-dimensional array called Q with six elements Q(0) to Q(5); and line 75 declares a one-dimensional array I of 100 elements I(0) to I(99) as well as a two-dimensional array J of 84 elements (4 rows, 0 to 3; and 21 columns, 0 to 20) from J(0,0) to J(3,20). Each array-name may appear in only one DIM statement which sets its maximum size throughout the program.

Note: Arrays not mentioned in any DIM are given a default upper limit of 10 - i.e. 11 elements (0) to (10) for a vector or 121 elements (0,0) to (10,10) for a matrix.

3.2.2 Matrix operations

A number of special matrix-handling statements are provided in Basic. They are described in Appendix E. We will not make a great deal of use of them, although MAT INPUT appears in the example in Section 3.3, but they are very convenient for certain numerical applications. The ones used in this book will be explained as they crop up.

3.3 Example program

This extract from a terminal session shows a listing and three runs of the program BUBBLE.XXX which sorts a series of numbers into ascending order by the 'bubble' or interchange method - 'bubble' because the higher numbers rise to the top like bubbles in a liquid.

The heart of the program is lines 220 to 320, and it involves a swapping process (lines 250 to 280). On line 250 it tests whether element J of vector X exceeds the next one, element J+1. If it does not, they are in order, and no swap is made. If it does, they are out of order, and a swap is made in lines 260 to 280 (and also counted on line 290). Notice that a temporary variable T must be used to hold one of the values or else it would be overwritten.

The inner loop using J (lines 240 to 300) performs one pass through the list as J increases from 1 to N-I. At the end of the first pass the last item must be the highest, at the end of the second pass the next-to-last item must be the second highest, and so on. So each pass can be shorter than the previous one, which is why the final value for J is N—I and not N—1. The outer loop (220 to 320) involving I controls the number of passes through the list. At most N—1, where N is the number of items, will be needed; but if C, the number of interchanges in the latest pass, equals zero, the list is already in order and the process can be finished early (line 310).

The remainder of the program is mainly concerned with input and output. Line 110 declares the vector X with 101 elements; lines 120 to 160 tell the user how MAT INPUT works; line 170 is a MAT INPUT statement for entering data into a vector; line 180 sets N to the number of data actually given; and 190 prints this on the terminal. (NUM is a special function - described in Appendix F - which yields the number of data given to the last MAT INPUT.)

Lines 360 to 380 use a simple loop to print the results. Notice the comma ending the PRINT statement on line 370, which causes the numbers to be printed 5 per line (not 1 per line). Line 400 indicates roughly how much work the program had to do.

LIS

```
BUBBLE.XXX    15:25              06-APR-76

100 REM**BUBBLE SORT:
110 DIM X(100)
120 PRINT "INPUT UP TO 100 NUMBERS FOR SORTING:"
130 PRINT "END LINE WITH & IF YOU HAVE NOT FINISHED AND
                                                  WANT"
140 PRINT "TO CONTINUE INPUT ON NEXT LINE."
150 PRINT "END LINE NORMALLY WITH RETURN AFTER LAST
                                                NUMBER."
160 PRINT "(ITEMS SEPARATED BY COMMAS ON INPUT.)"
170 MAT INPUT X
180 N=NUM               'NUM=NUMBER OF ITEMS GIVEN TO MAT
                                                  INPUT
190 PRINT N; "ENTRIES"
195 LET S=0    'TALLY OF ALL SWAPS
200 REM* NOW SORT THEM:
220 FOR I=1 TO N-1
230     LET C=0          'COUNT OF SWAPS THIS ROUND
240     FOR J=1 TO N-I
250     IF X(J) <= X(J+1) THEN 300
255     REM EXCHANGE X(J) AND X(J+1)
260     T=X(J)
270     X(J)=X(J+1)
280     X(J+1)=T
290     LET C=C+1                'ONE MORE SWAP
300     NEXT J
303     S=S+C   'ADD SWAPS THIS ROUND TO TOTAL
310     IF C=0 THEN 330          'DONE IF NO SWAPS THIS ROUND
320 NEXT I
330 REM*OUTPUT SECTION:
333 PRINT
340 PRINT "SORTED DATA:"
360 FOR I=1 TO N
370 PRINT X(I),
380 NEXT I
```

```
390 PRINT
400 PRINT "SWAPS =";S;" SWAPS PER ITEM = ";S/N
999 END

READY
RUN

BUBBLE.XXX    15:28            06-APR-76

INPUT UP TO 100 NUMBERS FOR SORTING:
END LINE WITH & IF YOU HAVE NOT FINISHED AND WANT
TO CONTINUE INPUT ON NEXT LINE.
END LINE NORMALLY WITH RETURN AFTER LAST NUMBER.
(ITEMS SEPARATED BY COMMAS ON INPUT.)
?1,2,3,4,5,6,7,8,9,0
10 ENTRIES

SORTED DATA:
0          1          2          3          4
5          6          7          8          9

SWAPS = 9 SWAPS PER ITEM = 0.9

TIME: 0.26 SECS.

READY
RUN

BUBBLE.XXX    15:30            06-APR-76

INPUT UP TO 100 NUMBERS FOR SORTING:
END LINE WITH & IF YOU HAVE NOT FINISHED AND WANT
TO CONTINUE INPUT ON NEXT LINE.
END LINE NORMALLY WITH RETURN AFTER LAST NUMBER.
(ITEMS SEPARATED BY COMMAS ON INPUT.)
?1,2,3,4,5,6,7,8&
?0,1,2,4,8,16,32,64&
?0,-1,-2,-3,-4,-5,-6,-7,-8&
?-99,99,100,101,1000
30 ENTRIES

SORTED DATA:
-99        -8         -7         -6         -5
-4         -3         -2         -1          0
 0          1          1          2          2
```

```
3          4          4          5          6
7          8          8          16         32
64         99         100        101        1000
SWAPS = 229  SWAPS PER ITEM = 7.6333

TIME: 0.48 SECS.

READY
RUN 170

BUBBLE.XXX    15:32           06-APR-76

?10,9,8,7,6,5,4,3,2,1,0
11 ENTRIES

SORTED DATA:
0          1          2          3          4
5          6          7          8          9
10
SWAPS = 55  SWAPS PER ITEM = 5

TIME: 0.25 SECS.
READY
```

The third run of this program (at 15:32) uses the RUN command followed by a linenumber (RUN 170). This starts the program at line 170, omitting the explanatory printout but not ignoring the DIM on line 110 which is not an executable statement but a declaration and which could have been placed anywhere before END.

3.4 Exercises

(1) Modify BUBBLE.XXX to print the numbers in descending order by changing line 360 not line 250. Use a STEP with a negative increment.

(2) Modify BUBBLE.XXX to print results in either ascending or descending order depending on an input from the user.

(3) The median of a set of numbers is that number which has the same number of values above and below it. In the set 0,3,9,18,7,5,4 the median is 5 which has 3 numbers above and below it. Write a program to compute the median of a set of input values. If it is given an even number of values, let it add the 2 middle values and divide by 2 to produce a median.

*(4) Write a program to compute the average deviation of a set of numbers. This is the sum of the differences of each number from the group mean, divided by the number of items in the group. Use the absolute

deviation, ignoring sign: this means that if the difference is negative the program should reverse its sign before adding it to the sum of deviations.

(5) Write a program that reads a series of exam scores (range 0 to 100) checks they are in the permitted range, and counts the frequency of each score using a vector, so that element 10 of the vector is the number of tests with scores of 10, element 24 is the number scoring 24, and sô on. Later modify it to print decile scores too - the number of scores in each range of ten, 0 to 9, 10 to 19, 20 to 29 . . . etc.

(6) Read in an N by M table and print out the highest and lowest value for every row and column, under suitable headings. Start with a small array (e.g. 2 by 4); later let it handle matrices up to 10 by 10.

(7) Read in an N by M table (N<=10, M<=20) and compute and print row and column totals and averages, under suitable headings.

*(8) Write a program to produce the Fibonacci series. This is the series 0,1,1,2,3,5,8,13,21,34 . . . where each term after the first pair is the sum of the two previous numbers. You will not need any arrays for this, nor necessarily any FOR or NEXT statements, although the process involves a loop. Stop the program when it has printed a number in the series greater than 100000.

4. Input and output

So far we have used INPUT (and MAT INPUT) and PRINT for all data transmission. INPUT is most useful for small quantities of data that vary from run to run of a program: for larger amounts of data that do not vary between runs, Basic provides the READ statement which reads information from DATA statements elsewhere in the program. PRINT is useful for relatively straightforward output and provides a certain degree of format-control: for complete control over the layout of printing, Basic provides the PRINT USING statement.

INPUT is very easy to use, and has been explained in Chapter 2. The only complication arises when you want to input strings of characters: this is covered in Chapter 6.

PRINT is also easy to use, and is very kind to the new programmer in the sense that it takes care of the details of the output format. As you advance, however, you will probably want more control over the appearance of your results. The rest of this section describes formatting with the PRINT statement. The additional facilities offered by the PRINT USING statement are described in Section 4.2.

Numbers are always justified to the left by PRINT and followed by one space. If the 6 most significant digits would not appear in decimal form, or if an integer is longer than 6 digits, then the number is printed in floating-point E notation. To have numbers output in other forms, you must employ PRINT USING.

Delimiters between items in the PRINT list are the comma, semicolon, and <PA>. Any of these may appear without intervening data items. The comma causes movement to the start of the next 14-character print zone; the semicolon causes no movement; and <PA> causes a 'form-feed' to the top of a new page. (On terminals without page-feed mechanism it merely causes 6 blank lines to be output.)

The TAB function may also be used to govern layout of results. The expression TAB(N) where N is any numeric formula can be an item in a PRINT list: it causes the printer to move on to position N in the output line. Thus

```
100 PRINT "A";TAB(20);"BC"
```

would print A in the first position and BC starting at position 20. If position N has been passed already however, the TAB function has no effect. Most terminals have 72 character positions, and the system normally inserts a carriage-return and linefeed if an attempt is made to print past the end of the line, so that it carries on at the start of a new line.

Other format-control statements are PAGE, NOPAGE and MARGIN which are described in Appendix B.

4.1 READ, DATA and RESTORE

The READ statement is used to assign to a list of variables values obtained from one or more DATA statements. Neither statement can be used alone without the other. READ causes the variables listed to be given, in order, the next available numbers from the collection of DATA statements. Before the program is run, the computer takes all the DATA statements in the order they appear and creates a block of data. Each time a READ is encountered during execution, the data block supplies the next available number or numbers. If the program attempts to read beyond the end of this block, it is halted with an OUT OF DATA message. It is important to realize that all DATA statements in a program together constitute one long stream of data. When a READ needs a new value, the next item is taken from this stream. So it is the order, not the exact position, of items in DATA statements that matters.

The location of DATA statements is arbitrary as long as they occur in the correct order: a common practice is to collect them all together and place them just before the END. (If execution reaches a DATA statement, nothing happens: it is ignored and control passes on to the next statement.)

A READ statement takes the form

linenumber READ list

where the list is a sequence of variables or array elements separated by commas. A DATA statement takes the form

linenumber DATA list

where the list is a sequence of constants (not formulas or variables) separated by commas.

It is obviously quicker to write

```
100 READ A,B,C,X,Y,Z
200 DATA -3,5,0,8.6667,2.105E-5,40
```

than to write

```
100 LET A=−3
110 LET B=5
120 LET C=0
130 LET X=8.6667
140 LET Y=2.105E−5
150 LET Z=40
```

although both have the same effect.

The RESTORE statement (just a linenumber and the word RESTORE) is used to re-read from the start of the data block. It is unnecessary at the start of a program, because the first data item read in a program will be the first constant in the first DATA statement - and then on sequentially. But it is useful if it is necessary to start scanning the data again from the beginning.

The MAT READ statement which reads data into an array is described in Appendix E. (Data may of course also be read into arrays without MAT READ.)

4.2 PRINT USING

The ordinary PRINT statement is satisfactory when you just want the results and are not too worried about their appearance: it removes from the programmer the burden of deciding exactly how the output should look. Eventually, however, a situation will arise where you want to decide precisely which characters should appear in what position on the output line, just how many digits should be printed after a decimal-point, and so on.

The PRINT USING statement lets the format of an output line to be governed by an 'image' of that line in the program. Its form is

linenumber PRINT USING image , list

where the list is a sequence of expressions for printing separated by commas, or by semicolons although this makes no difference to the output layout. (Strings may also appear in the list.) The image may either be a string or a linenumber. If it is a linenumber it refers to a line which consists of a colon (:) followed by a series of characters describing the form of the output. If it is a string, the string contains the same characters that would follow the colon on an image line. Thus

```
500 PRINT USING 505, A,X*2
505 :### ###.###
```

and

```
500 PRINT USING "### ###.##", A,X*2
```

both mean the same. Until we have dealt with strings in more depth (Chapter 6) we will normally use image lines rather than image strings.

Most of the characters in an image, including numerals, letters of the alphabet, and spaces, are printed as they stand; but some, including the number sign (#) and apostrophe (') have a special significance. For each item in the list following PRINT USING there will be a field, composed of these special characters, that describes its output format. When a PRINT USING is executed, the computer starts a new line of output and the first expression in the output list is printed in the form specified by the first field specification in the image. Then subsequent items are printed according to successive fields in the image, with any characters that are not part of a field specification being printed literally as they are encountered. If there are more expressions for output than fields in the image, a new line is begun and the image scanned again from the start. PRINT USING always writes a complete line: there is no way of suppressing carriage-return and line-feed at the end. (Current margin setting has no effect on PRINT USING, although an attempt to create a line of more than 132 characters will cause an error.)

4.2.1 Numeric field specifications

Numeric fields in the image describe the format of numeric expressions in the output list. They employ the number sign (#), the decimal point (.), and groups of four circumflexes (^^^^). Each number sign stands for a digit; the decimal point indicates the position of the decimal point, if any; and the four circumflexes, if present, reserve space for an exponent field - which always takes four character positions. Thus the value 123.456 would be printed in the various ways shown below with the following different field specifications.

Field specification	Output
###	123
###.###	123.456
##.##^^^^	12.35E+01

Note that automatic rounding (up or down as required) takes place and that numbers are justified to the right. Trailing zeroes are added if necessary so that there are always as many digits output after the decimal point as number signs after the decimal point in the image field. (A single number sign is treated as a printable character: two or more number signs specify a numeric field.)

An extra number sign will be required to reserve space for the minus sign if the quantity output is negative. If insufficient space is reserved for a number, an ampersand (&) is printed in the first position and the field widened to the right to accommodate it.

If a numeric field specification begins with two or more asterisks (**) instead of number signs, the number is printed with leading asterisks filling any unused positions. This is useful where a number must be protected so that additional digits cannot be added afterwards (e.g. for cheques). A solitary asterisk is treated as a printing character. Numbers output in this mode may not have an exponent field (see also Section 4.3).

If a field begins with two or more dollar signs ($$) the number is preceded on output by a 'floating' dollar. No spaces are left between the dollar sign and the number. Thus the field $$##.## would cause 123.456 to be printed as $123.46 and 1.23456 to be printed as $1.23. Dollar signs may replace two or more hashes in the specification. An isolated dollar in an image is treated as a printing character. Other currency symbols, such as the pound, are not available. Numbers output in this form may not contain an exponent part.

4.2.2 String field specifications

Strings as well as numeric expressions may appear in the output list. All string field specifications in an image begin with the apostrophe (') followed by a sequence of one of the four letters C,E,L or R. C calls for centering of the string in the output field; E calls for extension, to the right, to fit in all the characters of the string; L calls for the string to be justified to the left; and R calls for it to be justified to the right. If a string cannot be exactly centred (C) it will be one position off-centre to the left. If it is too large for the field it will be justified to the left and the characters furtherest right lost. If a string is too long for an E field, it is simply extended rightwards to accommodate all the characters. If a string is too big for an L field the characters furthest right are lost; and if it is too big for an R field the characters furthest right are also lost. Thus it is always the surplus characters on the right which are discarded if the string has to be truncated.) The number of characters in the field is the number of C's or E's or L's or R's plus one, for the apostrophe.

Thus the following lines

```
2000 PRINT USING 2001, "FIELDS", "ARE", "FOR", "SPECIES THAT
                                              THAT GRAZE"
2001 :THIS 'CCCC IS ''RRRRMAT 'LLLLFICATION
```

would produce

```
THIS FIELD IS A    FORMAT SPECIFICATION
```

as output. Notice that a single apostrophe causes only the first character of a string to be output.

Note: Image formatting is standard for numbers as described here; but beware of differences on other machines with string field specifications.

4.3 Example program

The following program (CHARGE.XXX) uses READ, DATA and PRINT USING, as well as the TAB function, to implement a rudimentary billing system - such as might be used on a much larger scale by the Gas or Electricity Board. The program reads data for a number of accounts and for each valid account produces a bill for the amount consumed. Each account consists of three numbers - an account number for identification, and two meter readings, past and present. If the program detects an error in these the account number is recorded for later printing; otherwise a bill is printed, according to a charging scheme whereby the first 100 units cost 1.775 pence per unit and subsequent units cost 1.02 pence. There is also a standing charge of £1.25.

Lines 100 to 150 initialize the program - line 150 reading from the first DATA statement the number of accounts to be processed. Lines 200 to 700 are the main loop of the program. In lines 230 to 270 the information for one account is read and checked. If it fails the tests on lines 240 to 270 (e.g. if the present meter-reading is lower than the previous one) execution passes on to the error section starting at line 400, which records the erroneous account number, and no bill is produced. But if the data passes the tests the program goes on to line 300 where the charges are worked out, then to line 500 where the actual printing takes place. In order to see the effects of the various PRINT USING and image statements in conjunction, examine the printout of the run at 17:20. Notice that one image (see line 600 and line 625) can be referred to in more than one PRINT USING statement. Notice also the effects of the TAB functions in lines 520 and 530, and the loop in lines 660 to 680 which divides up the invoices by printing a dashed line between them.

The data itself appears in DATA statements on lines 900 to 905. Line 900 indicates how many accounts are to be processed, and each line from 901 onwards contains the data for one account. In line 903 the past and present readings have been typed the wrong way round: the program detects this and lists the offending account number (44048) after it has finished printing invoices for the correct accounts. This could be corrected by getting the program into the working-area, re-typing line 903 as it should be, then re-running it. Other accounts could easily be added by inserting new DATA statements from line 906 onwards.

The importance of subjecting input data to a number of validation checks before processing it should not be underestimated. Programs that do not sufficiently scrutinize their input data before using it give computers a bad name by printing out absurdities like final demands for nought pounds and nought pence or sending pensioners the bill for their town's street lighting. Try to ensure that your programs apply every conceivable check to their data. Far better to have a program that grinds to a halt with no output except "DATA-FORMAT ERROR" than one which churns out acres of plausible yet spurious results. For it is results that are wrong but not obviously absurd which cause most trouble.

```
OLD CHARGE.XXX

READY
LIS

CHARGE.XXX   17:16             07-APR-76

1 REM*BASIC INVOICING PROGRAM:
100 DIM A(100)                  'LIST OF ACCOUNTS IN ERROR
110 LET E=0                     'NUMBER OF ERRORS
120 LET P1=1.775                'PENCE PER UNIT,1ST 100 UNITS
130 LET P2=1.02                 'PENCE PER UNIT, SUBSEQUENT
                                                      UNITS
140 LET C3=1.25                 'STANDING CHARGE (POUNDS)
150 READ A9                     'NUMBER OF ACCOUNTS
200 REM*MAIN LOOP:
210 FOR A0=1 TO A9
220    REM*INPUT AND CHECKING:
230    READ A,R1,R2             'ACCOUNT-NUMBER AND METER
                                                   READINGS
240    IF A<0 THEN 400          'ERROR
250    IF A>999999 THEN 400
```

```
260    IF R1>R2 THEN 400
270    IF (R2-R1)>9999 THEN 400       'SUSPICIOUSLY LARGE
300    REM*COMPUTE CHARGES:
310    U=R2-R1                   'UNITS USED
320    U2=U-100                  'UNITS AT LOWER RATE
330    IF U2>0 THEN 350
340    U2=0                      'NONE AT LOWER RATE
350    U1=U-U2                   'UNITS AT HIGHER RATE
360    C1=(P1*U1)/100            'PRICE IN POUNDS
370    C2=(P2*U2)/100
380    C=C1+C2+C3                'TOTAL INCLUDING FIXED
                                                 CHARGE
390    GOTO 500                  'PRINTOUT
400    REM*ERROR SECTION:
410    E=E+1                     'ONE MORE ERROR
420    A(E)=A                    'RECORD ACCOUNT-NUMBER
430    REM*WILL BE PRINTED LATER*
440    GOTO 700                  'SKIP PRINTING
500    REM*PRINTING SECTION:
510    PRINT
520    PRINT "ACCOUNT";TAB(16);"PREVIOUS";TAB(32);
       "PRESENT";TAB(45);"UNITS"
530    PRINT "NUMBER";TAB(16);"READING";TAB(32);
       "READING";TAB(45);"USED"
540    PRINT USING 550, A,R1,R2,U
550    :######       ######       ######       ####
560    PRINT
580    PRINT "CHARGES:"
590    PRINT USING 600, U1,P1,C1
600    :#### UNITS AT ##.## PENCE PER UNIT:
                          ****.## POUNDS
610    PRINT USING 600, U2,P2,C2
620    PRINT USING 625, "STANDING CHARGE", C3
625    :'LLLLLLLLLLLLLL                : ****.## POUNDS
630    PRINT USING 625, "TOTAL",C
650    PRINT
660    FOR I=1 TO 22
670       PRINT "-*";
680    NEXT I                    'UNDERLINE
690    PRINT
```

```
700 NEXT A0                    'NEXT ACCOUNT
750 REM*ERROR REPORT:
755 IF E<1 THEN 999
760 PRINT
770 PRINT "ACCOUNTS IN ERROR:"
780 FOR I=1 TO E
790 PRINT A(I)
795 NEXT I
800 REM*DATA FROM 900 ONWARDS:
900 DATA 5
901 DATA 1021,1,999
902 DATA 7071,0,1
903 DATA 44048,12794,11996
904 DATA 44049,72309,72381
905 DATA 44050,12138,12524
999 END
```

READY

RUN

```
CHARGE.XXX    17:20          07-APR-76

ACCOUNT       PREVIOUS       PRESENT        UNITS
NUMBER        READING        READING        USED
1021          1              999            998

CHARGES:
100 UNITS AT 1.78 PENCE PER UNIT:  ***1.78 POUNDS
898 UNITS AT 1.02 PENCE PER UNIT:  ***9.16 POUNDS
STANDING CHARGE                 :  ***1.25 POUNDS
TOTAL                           :  **12.18 POUNDS
-*-*-*-*-*-*-*-*-*-*-*-*-*-*-*-*-*-*-*-*-*-*

ACCOUNT       PREVIOUS       PRESENT        UNITS
NUMBER        READING        READING        USED
7071          0              1              1

CHARGES:
  1 UNITS AT 1.78 PENCE PER UNIT:  ***0.02 POUNDS
  0 UNITS AT 1.02 PENCE PER UNIT:  ***0.00 POUNDS
STANDING CHARGE                 :  ***1.25 POUNDS
TOTAL                           :  ***1.27 POUNDS
-*-*-*-*-*-*-*-*-*-*-*-*-*-*-*-*-*-*-*-*-*-*
```

```
ACCOUNT      PREVIOUS     PRESENT      UNITS
NUMBER       READING      READING      USED
44049        72309        72381        72

CHARGES:
 72 UNITS AT 1.78 PENCE PER UNIT:  ***1.28 POUNDS
  0 UNITS AT 1.02 PENCE PER UNIT:  ***0.00 POUNDS
STANDING CHARGE                 :  ***1.25 POUNDS
TOTAL                           :  ***2.53 POUNDS

-*-*-*-*-*-*-*-*-*-*-*-*-*-*-*-*-*-*-*-*-*-*

ACCOUNT      PREVIOUS     PRESENT      UNITS
NUMBER       READING      READING      USED
44050        12138        12524        386

CHARGES:
100 UNITS AT 1.78 PENCE PER UNIT:  ***1.78 POUNDS
286 UNITS AT 1.02 PENCE PER UNIT:  ***2.92 POUNDS
STANDING CHARGE                 :  ***1.25 POUNDS
TOTAL                           :  ***5.94 POUNDS

-*-*-*-*-*-*-*-*-*-*-*-*-*-*-*-*-*-*-*-*-*-*

ACCOUNTS IN ERROR:
44048

TIME: 0.72 SECS.
READY
```

4.4 Exercises

(1) Modify CHARGE.XXX by retyping line 903 correctly and by altering the price-rates set in lines 120 to 140 so that P1=18.5, P2=15 and C3=2.20, then re-run the program to see the effects.

(2) Change CHARGE.XXX so that it works in dollars and cents instead of pounds and pence - which will entail altering the image lines 600 and 625 to take advantage of the 'floating' dollar feature mentioned in Section 4.2.1. Also add the figures for some new accounts. Make them up yourself.

*(3) Calculate and print an interest table for investments showing the return on investments at from 1 to 12% over from 1 to 25 interest periods, using the formula R=(1+I/100)**N where R=return, I=interest rate %, and N=number of periods. Employ PRINT USING for the output.

(4) Type in and run the following program.

```
10 FOR X=1 TO 16
20    LET T=4 + X*4 - X*X/4
30    PRINT TAB(T);"*"
40 NEXT X
99 END
```

What does it do? How and why? Try replacing line 30 by

```
30 PRINT TAB(T);T
```

and also experiment with different formulas in line 20.

*(5) Write a program that accepts a list of frequencies and produces a histogram from them. It will probably be easier if the histogram is printed sideways. For instance, given the scores 0,7,3,19,2 . . . the program would produce something like:

```
01:
02: *******
03: ***
04: *******************
05: **
```

The final version of your program should be able to scale the input scores, so that if their range is greater than the available width of the paper (about 68 positions) the data are scaled to fit in.

(6) Write a program to print a square-root table for the numbers 0 to 99.9 in steps of 0.1 using the expression X**0.5 to give the square-root of X. You will almost certainly need PRINT USING for this one.

(7) Write a monthly billing program for a timesharing computer system where charges to users are: £5 per h of connected time; 10 per min of runtime; 12 p per disc block used; plus a standing charge of £5 per month. Data read are: user-number (up to 6 digits, not negative); connect-time in h; runtime in min; and average disc-block usage over the month. Typical test data could be:

```
9001 DATA 1021,29.1,24.4,327.5
9002 DATA 1111,30.9,25.7,96.6
9003 DATA 1141,25.6,440.0,75.2
9004 DATA 1161,30.0,76.4,69.8
9005 DATA 2461,8.0,1.6,500.7
9006 DATA 3111,13.6,4.8,197.0
```

(8) Write a weekly payroll program that for each of a number of employees reads in: (1) an employee code-number; (2) hours worked at the basic rate; (3) hours overtime worked; (4) 1 or 2 (for male or female). From this calculate the week's pay and deductions under the following assumptions: basic rate is £1.60 per h; overtime is £2.25 per h; men pay £1 a week in National Insurance; women pay 85 p per week National Insurance; tax-rate is 35% on each pound earned over 20 per week (i.e. tax-free allowance is £20 a week) and 50% on every pound earned over 100 in a week.

Reject input with negative hours worked or more than 144; and check input for other odd conditions. Produce payslips for each employee in the form shown below (where the number or star sign stands for one digit).

```
EMPLOYEE      HOURS WORKED              GROSS PAY     NET PAY
######        ###                       ****.##       ****.##

PAY:
BASIC RATE    ## HOURS AT 1.60 = ****.##
OVERTIME      ## HOURS AT 2.25 = ****.##
TOTAL                          = ****.##

DEDUCTIONS:
NATIONAL INSURANCE             = ****.##
INCOME TAX                     = ****.##
TOTAL                          = ****.##
```

Invent some data for the program and run it, revising it until it works to your satisfaction. Make the program stop when it finds a negative employee number.

5. Functions and subroutines

A routine is a segment of program to perform a given process which can be called from different parts of the main program. Basic provides two kinds of routines, subroutines and functions. Routines are useful whenever you want to break a long complex task into subtasks (sometimes called 'modules') that can be tested independently, then brought together to make a complete program.

It is not always possible to include every repetition of a given sequence of instructions within a loop, and a routine is a means of using the same process at places scattered throughout a program. Routines help make complex programs easier to write and to understand by dividing them into comprehensible parts, each with a relatively well defined job. They can also save you from 're-inventing the wheel': once you have a well-tested procedure to carry out a particular task (such as sorting a group of numbers into order) you can keep it on disc and incorporate it into a variety of programs.

Routines have two further advantages. They allow you to work with larger building-blocks than the elementary operations of the Basic language; and they allow you to express the hierarchical structure which many computations possess in a natural way. As you progress, routines become more and more useful. Eventually you will wonder how programs could be written without them.

5.1 GOSUB and RETURN

A subroutine is a section of code performing some operation that is required at more than one point in the program. To allow subroutines, Basic provides the GOSUB and RETURN statements. GOSUB transfers control to a specified linenumber, rather like GOTO. It is different from GOTO in that it also saves a return address so that the next RETURN causes a jump back to the statement immediately after the GOSUB. For example:

```
250 GOSUB 1000
255 REM: MAIN PROGRAM CONTINUES HERE
```

```
...
500 GOSUB 1000
505 REM: RETURN HERE AFTER 2ND GOSUB
...
1000 REM: START OF SUBROUTINE
1010 REM: PROCESS PERFORMED BY ROUTINE WOULD APPEAR
                                                 HERE
1099 RETURN          'END OF SUBROUTINE
```

shows a subroutine used at two places (lines 250 and 500) in a program. The RETURN at 1099 transfers control back to line 255 the first time the subroutine is called, from line 250, and returns to line 505 the second time, when it is called from line 500. In other words, the routine can be entered from various points and Basic keeps track of these so that RETURN sends execution back to the right place - the next statement after the one that called the routine.

Subroutines in Basic may be nested as long as they are not recursive, i.e. they may call other subroutines but may not call themselves either directly or by calling other routines which in turn call them. Basic subroutines do not have 'arguments' or local variables: they use the same variables as the main program.

Subroutines are generally placed near the end of a program. Some care must be taken not to enter a subroutine accidentally, by 'falling into' it rather than calling it with GOSUB. It is also necessary in Basic to guard against using variables in a subroutine which are in use for other purposes in the main program: it is quite easy, for instance, to start a FOR loop using I in a program and call a subroutine with a GOSUB within the loop which also uses I for another purpose. This sort of clash of variables can play havoc with a program! In order to avoid this you must be absolutely clear about which variables are altered in every subroutine. You will probably need to adopt some convention such as ending all variable-names with 9 (X9, Z9, Q9 etc.) in subroutines and never in a main program, and not relying on I or J as loop-counters over long stretches of program.

The example program in Section 5.4 shows GOSUB and RETURN in use.

5.2 Predefined functions

In addition to the standard arithmetic operators (described in Section 2.1.3) Basic includes certain elementary numeric functions. These are used in arithmetic expressions simply by writing their name (usually three letters) followed by an expression in brackets (the 'argument'), and yield the result of applying the function to the given argument. An example is the square-root function SQR. In the statement

```
300 LET R=SQR(A)
```

the square root of A is evaluated and assigned to R. So if A=49 the variable R would be set to 7, and likewise with other values of A. The argument of a function can be any arithmetic expression - although in the case of SQR a negative argument would cause an error. A slightly more complex example is

```
330 PRINT (X+SQR(X))/J
```

which instructs the computer to add X to its own square root, divide this value by J, and print the result.

In general, a function reference - which is the function name followed by a suitable argument expression in brackets - may appear wherever an arithmetic expression would be valid. It is another form of arithmetic expression.

A complete list of predefined functions available to the Basic user appears appears in Appendix F. Some of the most useful are also listed below.

Function	Result
ABS(X)	Absolute value of X, ignoring sign.
ATN(X)	Arctangent of X where X is in radians.
COS(X)	Cosine of X where X is in radians.
COT(X)	Cotangent of X where X is in radians.
EXP(X)	Natural exponent of X (e to the power of X).
INT(X)	Truncated value of X (largest integer <=X).
LOG(X)	Natural logarithm, base e, of X where X exceeds 0.
RND	Random fraction between zero and one.
SIN(X)	Sine of X where X is in radians.
SGN(X)	Returns +1 if X>0; 0 if X=0; and −1 if X<0.
SQR(X)	Square root of X where X is non-negative.
TAN(X)	Tangent of X where X is in radians.

The X indicates a numeric formula. The RND function requires no argument; but it requires a RANDOMIZE statement in the program to make it generate a new series of random numbers.

These functions are extremely useful in simplifying a number of calculations, especially those involving trigonometry. (To convert an angle in degrees to radians multiply by 180 and divide by pi.) They are part of the Basic system and do not have to be defined by the programmer.

5.3 User-defined functions

Functions may either be regarded as shorthand for long and complicated formulas or as subroutines that return only one value. The predefined functions have been dealt with above, and are listed in Appendix F.

The user may also define new functions with the DEF statement. User functions are named FNA to FNZ, i.e. FN plus one letter. For instance

```
50 DEF FNS(R) = 36/16.0934*R
```

defines a function called FNS with one argument, R, that converts a speed in metres per second to miles per hour. Given this definition the statement

```
500 LET X = FNS(V)
```

is equivalent to

```
500 LET X = 36/16.0934*V
```

because the expression V in the function reference replaces the argument R in the function definition. Here V is a simple variable, but it could be any arithmetic expression.

DEF is a mechanism for defining complicated expressions (with variable parts that are filled later) and naming them for use elsewhere in the program. The general form of a one-line function definition is

linenumber DEF FNa (list) = formula

where a is any letter; the list is a series of one or more arguments which conform to the same rules as variable names (i.e. a letter or letter plus digit); and the formula defines the function. If there is more than one argument in the list they are separated by commas. Usually the argument(s) on the left appear(s) in the formula on the right, but this is not strictly necessary. Any variables appearing in the formula on the right which are not arguments will have their current value at the time the expression is evaluated; while any arguments will have the value of the expressions that replace them in the function reference. Replacement is determined by position, not name: the Nth expression in the function reference replaces the Nth argument in the function definition. There is no necessary connection between argument-names and variable-names elsewhere in the program. Argument-names are local to the function definition in which they appear, and variables or arguments with the same name may appear in other parts of a program with different purposes.

If these concepts are puzzling, study the following example which prints a value (in this case e, the base of the natural logarithms) to a varying number of decimal places.

```
LIS

DIGITS          16:22          13-APR-76

1 REM*EXAMPLE OF FUNCTION DEFINITION:
10 DEF FND(N1,N2) = INT(N1*10^N2+0.5)/10^N2
15 REM*N1=VALUE, N2=NUMBER OF DECIMAL PLACES*
20 LET E=EXP(1)          'BASE E OF NATURAL LOGARITHMS
50 FOR D=0 TO 7
60     PRINT USING 88, FND(E,D)
70 NEXT D
88 :##.#######
99 END

READY
RUN

DIGITS          16:23          13-APR-76

3.0000000
2.7000000
2.7200000
2.7180000
2.7183000
2.7182800
2.7182820
2.7182818

TIME: 0.10 SECS.
```

The function defined in line 10 rounds a value (N1) to a given number of decimal places after the decimal point (N2). Notice that it uses the predefined INT function for truncation in the definition. This is perfectly legal. The function is used on line 60, with the values of E and D replacing the arguments N1 and N2 in the definition. The printout shows the value of E rounded to from 0 to 7 decimal places.

Functions with no arguments may also be defined in DEC10 Basic, in which case the bracketed portion is omitted entirely. They may also stretch over more than one line.

5.3.1 Multiple line definitions

Multi-line function definitions are ended by FNEND. The following is a multiple line function which gives the maximum of two numbers.

```
10 DEF FNM (A,B)
20 LET FNM=A            'RESULT IS A
30 IF A>=B THEN 50
40 FNM = B              'RESULT IS B
50 FNEND
```

Notice that the equal sign after the DEF is omitted, as is the defining formula. This is because the function is defined in terms of a sequence of instructions (lines 20 to 40), not a single expression. A multi-line function is termined by FNEND (which acts somewhat like RETURN in a subroutine). Somewhere in the function definition the function name has to be given a value: this is the result of the function. This is done in the above example by the LET statements on lines 20 and 40. Given this definition the statement

```
500 LET J=FNM(K,0)
```

would set J to the value of K or 0 - whichever is greater.

Function definitions may appear anywhere in a program. Generally they are put near the beginning. Transfers of control (with IF, GOTO etc.) are permitted within a multi-line function definition but not into or out of one: the function is called by putting its name (with appropriate arguments) in an expression, not by jumping into it. In fact if execution reaches a DEF statement it will be ignored, and so will any lines up to the FNEND.

User-defined functions in DEC10 Basic cannot take strings as arguments nor return a string as result.

Note: Many other Basic implementations do not allow multi-line function definitions.

5.4 Example program

The following program (TESTAT.XXX) employs two subroutines. The first, starting on line 1000, is a straightforward printing routine which is part of the program itself. The second, on lines 2000 to 2090, computes the mean, variance and standard deviation of a set of numbers. It uses the formula, which appears on line 2070,

```
V=(N*S2-S^2)/(N*(N-1))
```

where V is the variance, N is the number of items or scores, S2 is the sum of squares, and S is the sum. It is stored as a separate entity on disc under its own name (STATIS.XXX) and brought into the working area by the WEAVE command. The effect of this command can be seen by comparing the original listing of TESTAT.XXX (at 13:25) with the listing of lines 1000 to 9999 afterwards. Whereas the statistical routine is fairly general and could be used in a number of programs, the output routine, defined on lines 1000 to 1050, is relatively special-purpose, and is therefore not worth saving independently.

Both routines are used at two points in the program - the first time to compute and print the statistics for a set of data read from DATA statements, and then, if the user chooses, to do the same after transforming the data according to a function defined on line 20. Initially this is simply the natural logarithm function, but just before the second run of the program (at 13:30) the user redefines this by typing a new function on line 20 - whose effect is to express the data as percentages of the highest score (which is 202). It would be a simple matter to try various other transformation functions.

The data in lines 501 to 503 are all written as 3-digit numbers, with leading zeroes if necessary. This is not essential, but is done to make them easier to check visually.

```
OLD TESTAT.XXX

READY
LIS

TESTAT.XXX    13:25            03-MAY-76

1  REM*PROGRAM USING STATIS SUBROUTINE:
10  DIM A(100)
20  DEF FNT(X)=LOG(X)            'TRANSFORM FUNCTION
50  REM*GET DATA:
60  READ N                 'NUMBER OF DATA
70  MAT READ A(N)                'READS N ITEMS INTO ARRAY
80  GOSUB 2000             'STATS ROUTINE
90  GOSUB 1000             'PRINT ROUTINE
100  PRINT "DO YOU WANT DATA TRANSFORMED";
110  INPUT Y
120  IF Y=1 THEN 200
130  IF Y=0 THEN 250
140  PRINT "TYPE 1 FOR 'YES' "
```

```
150 PRINT "TYPE 0 FOR 'NO' "
160 GOTO 100
200 FOR J=1 TO N
210    A(J)=FNT(A(J))              'TRANSFORM DATA BY FUNCTION
220 NEXT J
230 GOSUB 2000                     'COMPUTE STATS
240 GOSUB 1000                     'PRINT RESULTS
250 STOP
500 DATA 36
501 DATA 013,011,054,005,047,070,098,097,102,109,088,037
502 DATA 020,045,067,093,054,040,147,202,192,180,156,090
503 DATA 060,083,065,058,072,084,094,095,110,097,093,089
1000 REM*PRINT ROUTINE:
1001 REM*EXPECTS N,M,V,S TO BE SET*
1010 PRINT
1020 PRINT "NUMBER", "MEAN", "VARIANCE", "STD. DEV."
1030 PRINT N,M,V,S
1040 PRINT
1050 RETURN
9999 END

READY
WEAVE STATIS.XXX

READY
LISNH 1000—9999
1000 REM*PRINT ROUTINE:
1001 REM*EXPECTS N,M,V,S TO BE SET*
1010 PRINT
1020 PRINT "NUMBER", "MEAN", "VARIANCE", "STD. DEV."
1030 PRINT N,M,V,S
1040 PRINT
1050 RETURN
2000 REM*ROUTINE FOR MEAN, VARIANCE AND STANDARD
                                          DEVIATION:
2001 REM*ALTERS S,S2,J9 VARIABLES*
2002 REM*EXPECTS DATA IN A(1:N) AND N AS NUMBER*
2010 LET S=S2=0
2020 FOR J9=1 TO N
2030    S=S+A(J9)                  'SUM
2040    S2=S2+A(J9)^2              'SUM OF SQUARES
```

```
2050 NEXT J9
2055 REM*NOW COMPUTE STATISTICS:
2060 M=S/N                       'MEAN
2070 V=(N*S2-S^2)/(N*(N-1))             'VARIANCE
2080 S=SQR(V)                    'STANDARD DEVIATION
2090 RETURN                 'RESULTS IN M,V,S
9999 END

READY
RUN

TESTAT.XXX     13:28          03-MAY-76

NUMBER         MEAN           VARIANCE        STD. DEV.
36             83.8056        2238.85         47.3165

DO YOU WANT DATA TRANSFORMED ?1

NUMBER         MEAN           VARIANCE        STD. DEV.
36             4.21082        0.619677        0.787196

TIME: 0.28 SECS.

READY
20 DEF FNT(X)=X*100/202
RUN

TESTAT.XXX     13:30          03-MAY-76

NUMBER         MEAN           VARIANCE        STD. DEV.
36             83.8056        2238.85         47.3165

DO YOU WANT DATA TRANSFORMED ?10
TYPE 1 FOR 'YES'
TYPE 0 FOR 'NO'
DO YOU WANT DATA TRANSFORMED ?1

NUMBER         MEAN           VARIANCE        STD. DEV.
36             41.4879        548.683         23.424

TIME: 0.32 SECS.

READY
```

In this example a new command (WEAVE) is introduced, and two new statements, STOP and MAT READ, as well as an extension of the LIS command (LISNH).

The WEAVE command specifies a file on disc and causes the contents of that file to be merged with the contents of the working-area. They are merged in linenumber order; and if a line of the incoming file has the same number as one already in the working-area it overwrites the one already there. This command is useful in cases where programs are built up from more than one piece. It is used above immediately after the listing of the main program TESTAT.XXX to bring in the subroutine filed as STATIS.XXX. Its effect can be seen from comparing the listing of the program before the WEAVE, without any subroutine starting at line 2000, with the listing of lines 1000 to 9999 afterwards. The subroutine has been inserted in the right place, making the program complete. (This method demands that you know the linenumbers of the separately stored routine or segment.)

The command LISNH 1000—9999 instructs the Basic system to list lines 1000 to 9999 of the working-area (inclusive) without any heading. The NH (no heading) can also be tacked on to the RUN command, giving RUNNH which runs the program with no preliminary heading. Sometimes the title, time and date at the top of a run or listing is a waste of time and space.

The STOP statement is used to halt the program at points other than the END. It is equivalent to a GOTO to the last line of a program, so that line 250 above could equally well have been GOTO 9999. MAT READ reads a whole array from DATA statements (see Appendix E).

Notice what happens when the user gives incorrect input to the program in the second run above. It rejects the erroneous input, and asks for it again.

5.5 Exercises

(1) Section 5.3.1 shows a function FNM which yields the greater of two numbers. Alter this so that it gives the smaller of two numbers.

(2) The function FNC below tests whether a value is an integer within a certain range. It returns a value 1 or 0 indicating whether the value is within range or not.

```
20 DEF FNC(N,A,Z)            'CHECKS N IS INTEGER FROM A TO Z
30 LET FNC=0               'ZERO MEANS OUT-OF-BOUNDS
40 IF N<>INT(N) THEN 80
50 IF N<A THEN 80
60 IF N>Z THEN 80
```

```
70 FNC=1                    'WITHIN RANGE
80 FNEND
```

Modify it so that instead it yields the input value itself if it is within range, or the nearest extreme if it is not. The function should be such that FNC(5,10,20)=10, FNC(15,10,20)=15, and FNC(25,10,20)=20.

(3) The following sub-routine takes a day-number (1 to 7) in D and prints the name of the corresponding day of the week (1=Monday). It employs the function FNC shown in the previous example. Write one which takes a month-number M and prints the name of that month, thus when M=9 it should print SEPTEMBER, and so on. Then use it in a program that accepts a number between 1 and 366 and prints the date of that day in the current year.

```
600 REM*WEEKDAY ROUTINE (D=DAYNUMBER):
610 IF FNC(D,1,7)=1 THEN 700
620 REM*CHECK INPUT WITH FNC FUNCTION*
650 PRINT "NO SUCH ";
660 GOTO 780
700 ON D GOTO 710,720,730,740,750,760,770
710 PRINT "MON";
715 GOTO 780
720 PRINT "TUES";
725 GOTO 780
730 PRINT "WEDNES";
735 GOTO 780
740 PRINT "THURS";
745 GOTO 780
750 PRINT "FRI";
755 GOTO 780
760 PRINT "SATUR";
765 GOTO 780
770 PRINT "SUN";
780 PRINT "DAY"
790 RETURN                  'WEEKEND
```

Notice the use of the ON statement: this directs control to one of a number of linenumbers depending on the value of a numeric formula, which is truncated to an integer if not integral (see Appendix B). After line 700 above execution will continue from line 710 if D=1, from line 720 if D=2, and so on. If D were less than one or greater than 7, the number of linenumbers in the list, an error would occur; but this is prevented by the test with FNC on line 610.

*(4) The following function is meant to simulate a dice-throw; that is, it should deliver a random integer from 1 to 6.

```
20 DEF FND = INT(RND*6)
```

It is not quite correct. Revise it so that it works properly. Write a short test program to check it.

(5) Define a Basic function with two arguments, an upper and a lower bound, which will give a random value evenly distributed between the two bounds. The result need not be an integer.

*(6) Tax is not levied on the first £875 of a person's annual income. It is levied at 35% on the next £4125 and at 50% on the remainder, over £5000. Write a function FNT such that FNT(P) is the tax levied on a yearly income of £P.

(7) Write a subroutine which strips duplicate items from a vector. It takes an input vector X (where X(0) indicates the number of elements in X) and produces an output vector X9 which is the same as the input except that duplicate items are deleted (with X9(0) indicating how many items remain in the new vector). Thus given

X(0)	X(1)	X(2)	X(3)	X(4)	X(5)	X(6)	X(7)
7	1	7	9	10	9	50	7

it should produce

X9(0)	X9(1)	X9(2)	X9(3)	X9(4)	X9(5)
5	1	7	9	10	50

as its result.

(8) Write a subroutine that finds at least 1 root of an equation, given by Y=FNA(X), within an interval from A to B, if any roots exist. The user should supply A and B.

The simplest method is probably repeated bisection of the interval in which the root is sought.

(9) Write a subroutine that uses Simpson's rule to calculate the area under a curve between two points X0 and X1. Assume that the function for generating the graph is FNA. That is, the height at point X is given by FNA(X).

In order to estimate an area with Simpson's rule: first divide the part to be measured into an even number of slices of width D by an odd number (N) of ordinates; then summate the heights of the curve at both ends (Y), the heights at the other odd ordinates (O) and at the even ordinates (E). The approximate area is then given by the formula

(Y + 2*O + 4*E) * (D/3)

which gains accuracy as the area is divided into thinner and thinner slices (until limited by the precision of the computer). For many common functions it gives an exact answer, e.g. polynomials of degree 3 or less.

(10) Write a complete integration program using the Simpson rule subroutine from the previous exercise, which will find the area under a curve of a user-defined function FNA between any two points supplied by the user.

6. Character strings

A string is a sequence of characters. So far we have only used string constants, which are sequences of characters normally enclosed in quotes. Thus we have been able to write statements such as

```
400 PRINT "THE ANSWER IS ";A
```

but have not been able to manipulate strings in any other way. The processing of non-numeric information is, however, an important area of computing; and Basic provides ample facilities for it.

A character, for our purposes, is one of the 128 separate symbols the computer can recognize. These include the letters A to Z, the digits 0 to 1 and various punctuation marks. A table of the characters which can be used in Basic is given in Appendix A. Notice that each character has a numeric code in the range 0 to 127.

Note: String-handling in Basic on machines other than the DEC10 may differ significantly from that described here. Apart from file processing (see Chapter 7), text processing is the area in which most differences between different versions of Basic occur. This is because neither string nor file processing was provided in the original Dartmouth Basic: they were grafted on later almost as an afterthought in various guises. Most modern varieties of Basic do have means of performing the operations described in this chapter, although possibly in other ways.

6.1 String variables and expressions

String variables can be used to hold string constants: they are named like numeric variables with a dollar sign appended, e.g. A$, A5$, Q2$ etc. A statement such as

```
10 LET B$ = "BASIC AS SHE IS SPOKE"
```

sets the current value of the string variable B$ to the string expression BASIC AS SHE IS SPOKE - in this case a constant of 21 characters including spaces.

One-dimensional string arrays are also permitted, which are vectors of strings. Thus

```
100 DIM Q$(60)
```

sets up a 61 element string vector, Q$(0) to Q$(60), and

```
200 LET A7$=Q$(7)
```

puts element 7 of Q$ into the string variable A7$. Two-dimensional string arrays, or matrices, are not allowed on the DEC system10 BASIC; and string vectors may not appear in MAT instructions.

The operations of multiplication, division etc. are obviously meaningless when applied to strings; but strings can be concatenated using the plus sign. Thus LET A$=B$+"ING" would put "STRING" into A$ if B$ contained "STR".

Strings can be compared in IF statements. The comparison depends on the rank order of their ASCII character codes (see Appendix A). The following are examples.

```
100 IF A$="YES" THEN 50
200 IF B$<"A" THEN 650
202 IF B$>"Z" THEN 650
```

The last two statements, lines 200 and 202, would test, in effect, whether the first character of B$ was alphabetic - going to line 650 if it was not. Trailing blanks are ignored in string comparisons so "NO"="NO " but leading blanks are not so " NO"<"NO". With strings composed entirely of letters < means 'earlier in the alphabet than' and > means 'later in the alphabet than'. With strings containing other symbols, it is necessary to know the ASCII code to determine the precise effect of string comparisons.

String constants that start with a letter and do not contain any commas, blanks or tabs need not be in quotes in DATA statements or in response to INPUT. Elsewhere they should be enclosed in quotes. (All strings may be in quotes.) Thus

```
500 DATA "DATE OF BIRTH", "2ND", OCTOBER, "1948"
```

contains four strings, three of which have to be in quotes because the first contains spaces and the other two start with a number. Note that "1948" could not be used in arithmetic expressions as it stands, although of course it can be printed and otherwise manipulated as a string: for instance, the relation "1948"<"1950" would be true in an IF statement.

There is no fixed upper limit on the length of a string, although in practice there are some problems with strings of over 132 characters.

6.2 The CHANGE statement

The simplest and often the most convenient way to access individual characters in a string is with the CHANGE statement. CHANGE A$ TO A converts the characters of A$ into a series of ASCII code numbers and puts them in the vector A. CHANGE A TO A$ does the reverse. Both forms of the CHANGE statement use element 0 of the vector to hold the number of characters in the string. The following example calculates and prints the frequency of each letter in an input string, using the CHANGE statement. (Non-alphabetic characters are counted but not printed out.)

```
LETTER          14:20               26-APR-76

1 REM*EXAMPLE OF CHANGE:
10 DIM V(64),C(127),X(1)
100 PRINT "GIVE A STRING PLEASE"
110 INPUT S$
120 IF LEN(S$)<65 THEN 150
130 PRINT "TOO LONG!"
140 GOTO 100
150 CHANGE S$ TO V
160 MAT C=ZER                'SET VECTOR C TO ZEROES
170 FOR I=1 TO V(0)
180     J=V(I)               'ASCII CODE WILL BE SUBSCRIPT
190     C(J)=C(J)+1          'ADD 1 TO CHARACTER-COUNT
200 NEXT I
250 PRINT
260 PRINT "CODE", "LETTER", "FREQUENCY"
275 LET X(0)=1               '1-ELEMENT ARRAY
300 FOR I=64 TO 90                     'LETTERS ONLY
310     IF C(I)<1 THEN 350             'SKIP IF NONE
320     X(1)=I
330     CHANGE X TO S$                 'SINGLE LETTER
340     PRINT I,S$,C(I)
350 NEXT I
999 END

READY
RUN
```

```
LETTER          14:22           26-APR-76

GIVE A STRING PLEASE
?"TO BE, OR NOT TO BE? THAT IS THE QUESTION."

CODE            LETTER          FREQUENCY
65              A               1
66              B               2
69              E               4
72              H               2
73              I               2
78              N               2
79              O               5
81              Q               1
82              R               1
83              S               2
84              T               7
85              U               1
TIME: 0.24 SECS.
```

The method employed is to tally the occurrences of each character-code in the corresponding position of the vector C. Thus C(65) contains the number of occurrences of the character whose code is 65 (the letter A) after the execution of the loop on lines 170 to 200; C(66) equals the number of B's, and so on.

It can be seen from line 110 that INPUT can obtain strings from the user, as well as numbers. READ and DATA likewise may be used with strings as well as numbers. This example uses, on line 120, the LEN function - which gives the number of characters in a string. It uses CHANGE on line 150 to put the ASCII numeric codes for the characters of S$ into the vector V, and the number of characters into V(0). It also uses CHANGE on line 330 to convert the single character code in the first element of vector X into a string (of one letter). One of the MAT instructions is also used on line 160 to fill the array C with zeroes (see Appendix E).

It should be clear from this program that the letters A to Z are represented consecutively by the numbers 65 to 90 in the ASCII code. The digits 0 to 9 are represented by the numbers 48 to 57. Although 128 characters, 0 to 127, are theoretically available, only the characters 32 (blank) to 95 (back-arrow) are likely to be useful to the Basic programmer.

6.3 String functions

The user may not define functions in Basic with strings as arguments or results, but a number of useful predefined string functions are provided. These are most helpful in manipulating substrings - i.e. breaking a string into parts, searching for one string within another one, and so on.

The LEN function which gives the number of characters in a string was used in the example in the previous section. Some other string functions are described below. (A complete list appears in Appendix F.)

CHR$(N) gives the character for which the numeric value N is the ASCII code. Thus CHR$(90)="Z" and CHR$(64)="@". N should be from 14 to 127. It will be truncated if not integral.

INSTR(A$,B$) searches for B$ within A$ and returns the character position in A$ where B$ starts, if found; otherwise zero. Thus INSTR("YESTERDAY","YES")=1, INSTR("YESTERDAY", "DAY")=7 and INSTR("YESTERDAY","TODAY")=0. An optional numeric argument may be used to specify starting position for the search: thus INSTR(8,"CATS EAT MEAT", "AT")=12 although INSTR("CATS EAT MEAT","AT")=2. If this argument is present it should be the first one.

LEFT$(A$,N) returns the first N characters of A$. Thus LEFT$("YESTERDAY",3)="YES".

MID$(A$,I,N) returns the substring starting at position I containing N characters in A$. If the last argument is omitted, it returns the whole string starting at I. Thus MID$("TOMORROW",4,2) ="OR" and MID$("TOMORROW",3)="MORROW".

RIGHT$(A$,N) returns the last N characters of the string. Thus RIGHT$("STRING",4)="RING".

SPACE$(N) returns a string of N spaces. Thus SPACE$(3)="   ".

Although Basic is primarily an introductory language, its string-handling facilities are quite powerful. It is possible to carry out some fairly sophisticated non-numeric computing in Basic, making it a general purpose, not just a mathematical, programming language.

6.4 Example program

In order to introduce string handling the following example involves both strings and numbers. The program NUMBER.XXX translates an input number into the words naming that number. For instance 8505 becomes EIGHT THOUSAND FIVE HUNDRED AND FIVE.

The program is written using two subroutines - one to separate a 3-digit number into 3 digits (hundreds, tens and units), starting at line 1000, which works by repeatedly dividing by 10 and saving the remainder, and another to translate a 3-digit number into words, starting at line 2000 - not because these routines are used at several places in the program but because this approach makes it easier to decompose the problem into manageable portions.

The number-naming words are stored in DATA statements from lines 101 to 105 (up to a hundred) and on line 110 (over a hundred). A total of only 30 are required. They are read into the string vectors A$ and B$ at the start of the program - in lines 200 to 240.

The conversion subroutine (lines 2000 to 2222) uses the routine starting on line 1000 to obtain 3 separate digits from the given number N. These are D(3) for the hundreds, D(2) for tens and D(1) for units. They are then used to address the appropriate number-naming words in A$() which are then concatenated with the current text in X$, the output string being assembled. Let us suppose that the input number (N) equals 125, and so that D(3)=1, D(2)=2 and D(1)=5, then the following is an abbreviated trace of its progress through this routine - which is the 'guts' of the program.

Line	Action	X$
2000	Enter, skip to 2005.	?
2005	Clear X$.	(null-string)
2010	Skip to 2020 because N is nonzero.	ditto
2020	Obtain hundreds, tens and units by calling subroutine at line 1000.	ditto
2030	D(3)=1 so proceed to 2035.	ditto
2035	D(3)=1 and so A$(D(3))=A$(1)="ONE";	ONE
	append "ONE"+"HUNDRED" to X$.	ONE HUNDRED
2040	Test whether AND is needed: it is.	ONE HUNDRED AND
2060	D(2)=2 so jump to 2080.	ditto
2080	Append A$(18+D(2))=A$(20) which is "TWENTY" to X$ with trailing blank.	ONE HUNDRED AND TWENTY
2085	D(1)=5 so proceed to 2090.	ditto
2090	A$(5)="FIVE", so append it to X$.	ONE HUNDRED AND TWENTY FIVE
2095	Exit	

The reader who wants to understand this routine and is still not clear from this trace just how it works is recommended to try following through some other 3-digit numbers to explore other paths through it.

From a partial solution, a routine which can handle numbers from 0 to 999, it is a short step to a more general solution, a program which can handle numbers from 0 to 999999999999 (albeit to only 8 significant figures), because numbers in this range can be rendered into words as

```
        '0–999' BILLION
        '0–999' MILLION
        '0–999' THOUSAND
(AND)   '0–999'
```

where a billion is 10E9. So if we can translate the '0–999', we can easily handle numbers of 12 digits by applying the routine for 3-digit numbers 4 times. (There are other problems, including deciding when 'and' is needed, but this is the essence of the solution.)

```
NUMBER.XXX    14:23            28-APR-76

1 REM*NUMBER - PROGRAM TO CONVERT NUMBERS TO WORDS:
2 REM*WILL ACCEPT NUMBERS UP TO 12 DIGITS
3 REM*ACCURATE UP TO 8 SIGNIFICANT FIGURES*
10 DIM A$(27),B$(4),S(4)
100 REM*DATA WORDS:
101 DATA ONE,TWO,THREE,FOUR,FIVE
102 DATA SIX,SEVEN,EIGHT,NINE,TEN
103 DATA ELEVEN,TWELVE,THIRTEEN,FOURTEEN,FIFTEEN
104 DATA SIXTEEN,SEVENTEEN,EIGHTEEN,NINETEEN,TWENTY
105 DATA THIRTY,FORTY,FIFTY,SIXTY,SEVENTY,EIGHTY,NINETY
110 DATA THOUSAND,MILLION,BILLION
150
200 REM*GET DATA:
210 FOR I=1 TO 27
220     READ A$(I)
225 NEXT I
230 LET B$(1)=" "
240 READ B$(2),B$(3),B$(4)
245
250 REM*CONVERSION:
260 PRINT "GIVE A NUMBER PLEASE";
270 INPUT N
```

```
280 IF N<0 THEN 9999              'STOP IF NEGATIVE
290 LET Q=N-INT(N)                'FRACTIONAL PART -> Q
295 IF N>=1 THEN 315
300 PRINT "ZERO"                  'NOUGHT IS SPECIAL CASE
310 GOTO 480
315 LET N=INT(N)                  'TRUNCATE N
320 LET Q1=N-100                  'WHETHER OVER 100
325 FOR K=1 TO 4
330 X9=N/1000-INT(N/1000)
333 REM*S() GETS BILLIONS,MILLIONS,THOUSANDS,UNITS*
340 S(K)=INT(X9*1000+.5)
350 N=INT(N/1000)
360 NEXT K
365
370 FOR K=4 TO 1 BY -1
380     N=S(K)             '3-DIGIT NUMBER
390     IF N<1 THEN 470           'IGNORE NIL
400     GOSUB 2000                'NUM->STR
410     IF K>1 THEN 450
420     IF N>99 THEN 450
430     IF Q1<1 THEN 450
435     REM*TESTED IF 'AND' NEEDED*
440     PRINT "AND";
450     PRINT X$;" ";             'PRINT WORDS
460     PRINT B$(K)               'B$(1) IS NULL
470 NEXT K
472
475 REM*FRACTIONAL PART, IF ANY:
480 IF Q<=0 THEN 500
490 PRINT " AND A BIT"
500 GOTO 250                      'NEXT INPUT
505
1000 REM*ROUTINE TO SPLIT 3DIGIT NUMBER INTO 3 DIGITS:
1001 REM* INPUT IS N : OUTPUT IS D(1-3) *
1002 REM* USES VARS X & D9, AND J AS COUNTER *
1005 IF N<0 THEN 1066
1006 IF N>999 THEN 1066 'OUT OF RANGE
1010 LET X=N            'MAKE COPY OF N
1015 FOR J=1 TO 3
1020     D9=X/10-INT(X/10)
```

```
1025      D(J)=INT(D9*10+0.5)
1030      X=INT(X/10)
1035 NEXT J
1050 REM* OUTPUT IN D(1-3)*
1060 RETURN              'N NOT ALTERED
1066 PRINT N;" OUT OF BOUNDS (0-999)"
1077 STOP
1100
2000 REM* ROUTINE TO CONVERT DIGITS TO WORDS:
2001 REM* INPUT IS N : OUTPUT IS X$ *
2002 REM* NUMBER-NAMES IN A$(1-27)
2005 LET X$=""           'CLEAR X$ (TO NULL)
2010 IF N<>0 THEN 2020
2012 X$="NOUGHT"
2015 RETURN
2020 GOSUB 1000                   'SPLIT N INTO DIGITS
2030 IF D(3)<1 THEN 2050          'NO HUNDREDS
2035 X$=A$(D(3))+" HUNDRED "
2040 GOSUB 2200                   'TEST FOR AND
2050 IF D(2)<1 THEN 2085          'NO TENS
2060 IF D(2)>1 THEN 2080
2066 REM* TEENS HERE*
2070 X$=X$+A$(D(2)*10+D(1))
2075 RETURN
2080 X$=X$+A$(18+D(2))+" "
2085 IF D(1)<1 THEN 2075
2090 X$=X$+A$(D(1))
2095 RETURN
2200 REM*SUBSUB ROUTINE*
2202 IF D(1)+D(2) < 1 THEN 2222
2220 X$=X$+"AND "
2222 RETURN
9999 END

READY
RUN

NUMBER.XXX   14:28              28-APR-76

GIVE A NUMBER PLEASE ?1976
ONE THOUSAND
NINE HUNDRED AND SEVENTY SIX
```

```
GIVE A NUMBER PLEASE ?777.7
SEVEN HUNDRED AND SEVENTY SEVEN
AND A BIT
GIVE A NUMBER PLEASE ?1234567
ONE MILLION
TWO HUNDRED AND THIRTY FOUR THOUSAND
FIVE HUNDRED AND SIXTY SEVEN
GIVE A NUMBER PLEASE ?12000000000
TWELVE BILLION
GIVE A NUMBER PLEASE ?1234567.89
ONE MILLION
TWO HUNDRED AND THIRTY FOUR THOUSAND
FIVE HUNDRED AND SIXTY SEVEN
AND A BIT
GIVE A NUMBER PLEASE ?9876543210
NINE BILLION
EIGHT HUNDRED AND SEVENTY SIX MILLION
FIVE HUNDRED AND FORTY THREE THOUSAND
TWO HUNDRED AND FIFTY
GIVE A NUMBER PLEASE ?16094
SIXTEEN THOUSAND
AND NINETY FOUR
GIVE A NUMBER PLEASE ?13
THIRTEEN
GIVE A NUMBER PLEASE ?-1

TIME: 0.56 SECS.
READY
```

The subroutine starting at line 2000 makes extensive use of concatenation (with +) to build up a phrase in X$.

Notice that precision is lost in numbers of over 8 digits, but that the most significant 8 figures are preserved.

6.5 Exercises

(1) Write a program to perform a bubble-sort (into alphabetic order) on a vector of strings.

(2) Write a program to produce a table of all the usable character codes (32 to 95) in Basic and their character equivalents. The output should be in two pairs of columns, to fit on a page (rather like Appendix A).

(3) Revise LETTER (shown in Section 6.2) to read several strings from DATA statements and accumulate tallies for them all: use as test data the first 15 lines of this chapter, 1 line to 1 string. Your revised program should print the letter frequencies for the whole 15 lines. The letters E and T should be very common. Later, extend it to calculate percentages as well.

(4) Extend NUMBER.XXX so that it deals with fractions as well. Thus instead of rendering 77.851 as SEVENTY SEVEN AND A BIT it should print SEVENTY SEVEN POINT EIGHT FIVE ONE. This is not too hard since decimals are spoken one digit at a time.

(5) Write a Basic program to accept a string containing several words, separated from one another by one or more blanks, and to produce as output the number of words in the string and a string composed of the initial letters of each word. Given "BASIC AS SHE IS SPOKE" it should print 5 and BASIS.

*(6) Suppose the vectors A$(1:N) and B$(1:M) both contain words in alphabetic order. Write a program to merge the two into a single alphabetic vector C$.

(7) Write a program to read a length of text from DATA statements and calculate letter-pair frequencies. Treat all non-alphabetic characters as equivalent ('@' is suggested). Accumulate the frequencies in a matrix C of dimension (26,26) - so that C(1,1) is the frequency of the pair AA, C(26,5) is the frequency of ZE, C(0,2) is the frequency of @B where @ stands for any non-alphabetic character, and so on. It should print only the non-zero entries - i.e. those letter pairs that actually occur.

(8) Write a subroutine using the CHANGE statement to reverse the order of the characters in a string. Given "BASIC" as input its output should be "CISAB".

*(9) Write a subroutine to reverse a string which does not use the CHANGE statement. Then write a program to use it, as well as the version using CHANGE from the previous exercise, many times to compare the two methods in efficiency.

(10) Write a program that gives the user instruction in Basic. It accepts a Basic keyword (e.g. LET, PRINT etc.) from the keyboard and either prints a standard format and examples of that statement-type or else responds: KEYWORD NOT RECOGNIZED.

(11) Write a program to convert from verbal to numeric representation so that, for example, ONE HUNDRED AND NINETY becomes 190. This is the reverse of NUMBER.XXX. It is not easy.

(12) Write a program to read, and check, Roman numerals between I and M and print out their modern equivalents. Thus CIV as input should cause 104 as output. This is extremely difficult!

7. Datafiles

So far the only means we have had of storing data permanently between runs of a program is in DATA statements. However information in DATA statements is not easily shared by different programs, and large quantities of such data can make a program excessively bulky.

Information not specifically belonging to a single program may be held for long-term storage on a 'file'. Files are usually held on disc, and are referred to in Basic programs by a channel-number which is assigned to the named file by a FILE or FILES statement.

There are two types of datafile in DEC10 Basic - sequential and random-access. Sequential files can be subdivided into those with or without linenumbers; and random-access files can be subdivided into those containing numbers or those containing strings. The channel-number identifying a file is preceded by a number-sign (#) if it is sequential, and by a colon (:) if it is a random-access file. Nine channels (1-9) may be in use at any one time.

Sequential files can only be processed in serial order from the beginning; whereas random-access files are divided into 'records' each of which can be accessed individually. It is not possible to start reading or writing a sequential file from anywhere except the beginning. There is no way, for example, to read up to a particular point on a sequential file and then start writing on it from there. For this sort of processing a random-access file must be used.

Unfortunately, file-handling is the area where the most pronounced differences between versions of Basic are found. Users of other Basic systems can gain some general principles from this chapter, but for technical details will have to turn their attention to the manufacturer's manual. (File-handling is not normally the province of the inexperienced programmer.)

7.1 Sequential files

7.1.1 Linenumbered files

The easiest kind of file to start using is a linenumbered sequential file, because such files can be set up and edited from the terminal in the same manner as Basic programs. (In fact, a saved Basic program is one example of a sequential linenumbered file.)

The following dialogue creates a linenumbered sequential file called DATA.BAS containing names, initials and birthdates.

```
READY

NEW DATA

READY

10  OLD,MRS.V.,1,JAN,1900
20  SMITH,DR.J.C.,15,MAR,1940
30  FORSYTH,MR.R.S.,2,OCT,1948

SAV

READY
```

The rules for data-items on a line are similar to those for DATA statements: a comma, tab or space(s) may be used to separate items, and strings need only be in quotes when they start with a non-alphabetic character or contain separator characters such as commas or blanks. At least one space (or tab) must separate the linenumber from the first data-item. Thus each line of the above file contains three strings (name, title and month) and two numbers (day and year). A program statement to read one line of this file might be

```
500  READ#1, N$,I$,D,M$,Y
```

assuming it had been assigned to channel 1.

Note: A line of a sequential file is not the same thing as a record of a random-access file. As in DATA statements, all the items in a sequential file form one continuous stream of data, and are read one by one. The distribution of items per line is arbitrary (although no line may be over 142 characters) and is ordinarily chosen for convenience.

7.1.2 Channels and files

Correspondence between files and channels may be set up in two ways. The FILES statement assigns files to channels during compilation, before execution; while the FILE statement assigns files to channels when the program is running. The FILES statement takes one or more file specifications as arguments, separated by commas or semicolons, and assigns them to channel-numbers in the order in which they appear. Up to nine may be allocated in this way, and channels may be skipped by putting nothing between a pair of commas. For instance

```
100 FILES MARX.ISM,DATA.BAS,,F1.DAT
101 FILES FIVE
```

puts MARX.ISM on channel 1, DATA.BAS on channel 2, nothing on channel 3, F1.DAT on channel 4, and FIVE.BAS on channel 5. Note that the extension BAS is assumed if none is given and that files are assumed to be sequential unless specified as random-access.

If no file exists with a given name and extension a new file of that name will be opened on your disc area. Thus a Basic program can create new files as well as reading, amending or extending old ones.

The FILE statement takes effect when executed, and can be used to change channel allocation while the program is running. Its argument is a channel-number preceded by the # (or : for random-access files) and followed by a comma then a string formula naming the file. Thus the file name should be in quotes if it is a literal. For example

```
550 FILE#8, "INPUT"
575 FILE#9, A$+".DAT"
```

would assign INPUT.BAS to channel 8 and OUTPUT.DAT to channel 9, assuming that A$ contained "OUTPUT" when statement 575 was executed. A common use of FILE is illustrated below.

```
200 PRINT "WHICH FILE PLEASE";
210 INPUT F$
220 FILE #2, F$
225 IF END#2 THEN 250
230 READ #2, A$,B$,N,X(N),C2$
240 IF A$="TARGET" THEN 500          'FOUND IT
245 GOTO 225
250 REM: TARGET NOT FOUND – PROGRAM CONTINUES
```

If a file had already been open on channel 2 before this section of program was reached, it would be closed (with no loss of data) before the file specified by F$ was opened on channel 2.

7.1.3 Reading and writing sequential files

The READ and WRITE statements are used to transfer information to and from line-numbered sequential files. Their first argument is a channel specifier followed by a list of variables (READ) or formulas (WRITE). For instance

```
100 READ #2, A(I),B(I),N$,P1
```

would read two numbers, a string, then another number from the linenumbered sequential file on channel 2; and

```
200 WRITE#J, I,A(I),2*B,SQR(X/Y)
```

would write the values of I, A(I), 2*B and the square-root of X/Y on to the file on channel 5 (assuming J=5).

READ expects each line in the file to start with a linenumber, which it ignores. WRITE begins each new line with a linenumber followed by a tab - the first line being numbered 1000 and subsequent linenumbers being incremented by 10. Each WRITE in the program writes one line in the file.

INPUT and PRINT have the same format as READ and WRITE but do not expect linenumbers. If INPUT encounters a linenumber it will be treated as numeric data. INPUT and PRINT are for use with non-linenumbered files. Examples are shown below.

```
300 INPUT #1, N,A$(N)
333 PRINT #2, A$(I);I**2
```

The PRINT on line 333 shows that layout conventions such as separating items by semicolons instead of commas for closer spacing can be used in WRITE or PRINT statements to sequential files. The TAB function can also be used. (Closely-packed output will save disc space.)

Remember that, for all files, numbers must be read into numeric variables (or array-elements) and strings into string variables. The consequences of trying to read a number into a string variable can be unpredictable, and the consequences of trying to read a string into a numeric variable are usually disastrous.

7.1.4 RESTORE and SCRATCH

In order to read or write an already open file from the beginning again, it is necessary to use RESTORE (for reading) or SCRATCH (for writing). Thus

```
50 RESTORE#4, #J+2
```

would prepare to read from the beginning of the file on channel 4, and on channel 6 assuming J=4. Likewise

```
60 SCRATCH #7, #ABS(A/2)
```

would prepare to write from the beginning of the files on channels 7 and 8 (assuming A=16 or A=−16) by erasing their current contents if any and re-setting their pointers to the start. (All files are in a RESTOREd state at the start of a program.)

In order to change from reading to writing a sequential file in a program it is necessary to use SCRATCH, and to change from writing to reading it is necessary to use RESTORE. It is an error to try to read from a file you have been writing on without an intervening RESTORE, or to try to write on a file you have been reading from with no intervening SCRATCH.

7.1.5 End of file

To test for the end of a sequential file when reading from it, use IF END. Thus

```
950 IF END #3 THEN 9999
```

transfers control to line 9999 if there is no more data to be read on channel 3. IF END only tests when executed: it does not set a test that remains in force until a new one is set as in some other versions of Basic. An error will result if you use IF END on a sequential file that is in 'write mode' - i.e. one which has been subject to WRITE or PRINT or SCRATCH and not subsequently RESTORE.

7.1.6 Output format

Since sequential files may be listed on the terminal or lineprinter it is possible to use them for printed reports, and so there are several facilities for making them more legible. PRINT USING (or WRITE USING for linenumbered files) may be employed on sequential files for greater format control. The form is PRINT#N USING I, . . . or WRITE#N USING I, . . . where N is a channel-number and I an 'image' reference, and the dots signify an output list. It is also possible to use QUOTE and NOQUOTE (see Appendix B) on sequential files so that strings are, or are not, enclosed in quotation-marks if they start with a number or contain separator characters. QUOTE mode is suitable for files that are later to be read back by a Basic program. NOQUOTE mode is suitable for files that are destined for printing as reports or such-like. NOQUOTE is the default setting at the start of a program.

It is also possible to divide output to sequential files into pages of a given length using the PAGE statement. (See Appendix D.) Note that one line of a sequential file may not contain more than 142 characters; and for lines longer than 72 characters it is necessary to use MARGIN to specify a non-standard page-width.

7.2 Random-access files

7.2.1 Opening random-access files

On the DEC System-10 Basic random-access files are divided into records of fixed length, each of which can be accessed individually. Associated with each channel is a 'pointer' indicating the current record, and this can be tested or altered by the program in order to gain access to any particular record. The pointer determines which record will be read or written next. Records can be read or written freely at any point in a random-access file, in any order (in contrast with the rules for sequential files). A random-access file may contain strings, or numbers, but not both.

Random-access files are assigned to channels by the FILE or FILES statements, using a colon (:) in place of the number sign (#) and following the filename with a type-sign - which is $ if the file is for strings or % if it is for numbers - and then, if it is for strings, the number of characters per record, which must not exceed 132. Thus

```
20 FILES INPUT.DAT$64, RANDY%
25 FILE :4, "STRAND$", :8, "RAX.FIL%"
```

would open a random-access string file called INPUT.DAT with record-length of 64 characters on channel 1; a numeric random-access file called RANDY.BAS on channel 2; a random-access string file, STRAND.BAS, on channel 4; and a numeric random-access file called RAX.FIL on channel 8. The record-size for STRAND.BAS would be 34 characters - the default value if none is given. For numeric files the record-length is always one number, so individual numbers can be accessed directly, almost as if the file were an array. (Notice that the BAS extension is assumed if none is specified.)

7.2.2 Manipulating the pointer

The SET statement, together with the LOC and LOF functions, enables the programmer to manipulate the file-pointer to process particular records. SET takes the form SET :N,M where N is the channel-number and M the new pointer value. Both may be any arithmetic expressions, but will be rounded down to integers if necessary; and if N>9 or N<1 an error will result. For example

```
100 SET :5, J+1
```

sets the pointer for channel 5 to the J+1th record. SET can take more than one pair of channel-number and pointer-location formulas, as in

```
120 SET :5,J+2, :N,20
```

which sets the channel 5 pointer to J+2 and the channel N pointer to 20. (N should be from 1 to 9 and should refer to a channel that does have a random-access file assigned to it.)

The predefined function LOC takes a channel-number as argument and returns the number of the current record, i.e. the current pointer value, for the file on that channel. Thus

```
200 SET :4,LOC(4)+10
```

shows the pointer for channel 4 being reset to 10 more than its previous value, which might be used to process every tenth record in that file.

LOF takes a channel-number as its argument and gives the number of the last record in the file on that channel which contains data. Thus

```
250 IF LOC(N) > LOF(N) THEN 500
```

has the same effect as

```
275 IF END :N THEN 500
```

since both jump to line 500 if the channel N pointer points beyond the last entry on the file.

7.2.3 Reading and writing random-access files

RESTORE and SCRATCH may be used on random-access files, although they are not mandatory. RESTORE :N sets the channel N pointer to the first record; SCRATCH :M does the same for the random-access file on channel M, and erases its current contents. (Be careful never to SCRATCH a file you really want to keep.)

READ and INPUT are equivalent when used on random-access (as opposed to sequential) files. Both start reading at the current record as indicated by the pointer and continue sequentially until all the variables in the input list are filled, leaving the pointer indicating the next record after the last one read. WRITE and PRINT are also equivalent for random-access files: they start writing at the current record and continue sequentially until all the values in the output list have been transferred to the file, leaving the pointer pointing one beyond the last item written. This means that it is easy to read and write a random-access file serially. It is, in fact, quicker than processing a sequential file and may be used unless the features of sequential files (printability, mixing of strings and numbers on one file, ease of editing etc.) are required.

READ, WRITE, INPUT and PRINT have the same format for random-access files as for sequential ones, except that the number sign (#) is replaced by the colon (:), as in the following examples.

```
808 READ :5, X,J,A(J)
888 PRINT:6, A$,LEFT$(Z$,4)
```

Note that strings and numbers cannot be mixed in input or output lists, and that format-control characters cannot be used. Note also that you cannot read beyond the last record containing data in a random-access file, although you can of course write beyond it, thus extending the file or even creating 'gaps' of records which contain no data before the last entry in the file. If you read such gaps their value is zero in numeric files, or the null string of no characters in string files.

7.3 Further points

It is not possible to use MAT PRINT or MAT READ on files. In order to transfer a vector or matrix to or from a file, you must transfer the elements individually, generally by means of a FOR/NEXT loop.

Sequential files may readily be processed by programs external to the Basic system, but random-access files are not in a suitable format for this and generally can only be processed by Basic programs. Sequential files may also be listed on the terminal.

Unfortunately, there is no way of testing, in DEC Basic, whether the next item to be read from a sequential file is a string or a number. Thus although strings and numbers may be mixed on one file, the programmer must know their order, or insert markers to inform the program what type of data comes next. (Alternatively, all numbers can be stored as strings and converted with the VAL function after being read. See Appendix F.)

File-processing is a large, important and sometimes complex topic. Only the major points are covered in this chapter. Further information about file-manipulating statements is given in Appendix D.

The great advantage of having your data filed on disc (in a 'databank') is that once it is there you can do practically anything with it, restricted only by the limits of your own imagination. However, when you get to the stage of doing complex processing on large files in Basic, you are probably ready for a more 'grown-up' programming language.

7.4 Example program

The following program (WORDCT.XXX) reads words one at a time from a linenumbered sequential file on channel 3 and writes all the different words, and their frequencies, on to two random-access files - one (OUT1) for strings and the other (OUT2) for numbers. It employs a 'hash-coding' technique. Hash-coding (or 'scatter-storage') is a method for allocating entries to store locations where the entries arrive in unpredictable order. Some property of the incoming entry is used to decide where to place it. In this case the entries are words, and the initial letter of a word determines where it will be put. Thus the program will try to store words beginning with A at record 1 of OUT1 onwards, words starting with B at location 13 onwards, and so on. The hashing function is defined on line 50. Clearly many words may be allocated to the same place; but if that place/record is already in use the program steps through subsequent records until it finds a free one - which is where the new word is stored.

The point of this is that the presence or absence of an entry on the file can be ascertained fairly quickly because, given a word, the program knows where to start looking for that word; and in this application it has to decide for each incoming word whether it has met it before. If the (growing) file of words already met were unordered, the whole file would have to be searched every time a new word was read to discover that it had not so far been encountered, and, on average, half the file would be searched to find out that an input word had been read before. This would be grossly inefficient. (Hasing, too, becomes inefficient when the hash table, or file, is over half full.)

There follows a step-by-step outline of the logic of the hash-storage method. Linenumbers of the program which correspond to this algorithm have been inserted, where appropriate, in square brackets after each step.

(1) Enter [150].

(2) Get input item (A$) [160 to 190].

(3) Compute key from value of item (K) [200 to 230].

(4) Examine item at position K [250 to 270].

(5) If it is empty go to step 6; otherwise go to step 8 [280].

(6) The item is new: insert it at location K, and set the associated counter to 1 [360 to 400].

(7) Go to step 13 [410].

(8) Does the input item (A$) match the item at position K (B$)? If so go to step 9; otherwise go to step 10 [285].

(9) The item is already stored: leave it, and increment its associated counter by 1; then go to step 13 [300 to 350].

(10) Continue the search at the next location: increment K by 1 [290].

(11) If K is greater than maximum, set K back to 1 (and if this happens more than once the table is full).

(12) Go back to step 4 [295].

(13) Exit.

If a string vector rather than a string file had been used to store the words, processing time would have been reduced; but the use of a file permits the program to operate on much bigger input texts. A string array of 400 elements would fit in the working-area; but one of 4000 elements would make the program too big to run, while a file of that size would not be inordinately large. (For a larger file, of course, the scattering function would need to be altered to distribute entries evenly - as far as possible - over the increased space available.)

```
WORDCT.XXX    14:13               03-MAY-76

1 REM*WORD-COUNT PROGRAM:
10 FILES OUT1$16, OUT2%
12 REM*RAX FILES FOR WORDS AND TALLIES*
15 SCRATCH :1, :2
20 DIM A(16)
50 DEF FNH(X)=ABS(X-65)*12           'HASH FUNCTION
60 REM*FILL 400 RECORDS OF OUT1 & OUT2 WITH BLANKS:
65 FOR I=1 TO 400
70    PRINT :1, " "
75    PRINT :2, 0
80 NEXT I
100 REM*GET INPUT FILE:
110 PRINT "GIVE INPUT FILE.EXT PLEASE"
120 INPUT A$
130 FILE #3,A$
140 LET N=L=W=0 'SET COUNTERS TO NIL
150 REM*NEXT WORD:
160 IF END#3 THEN 500
170 READ #3, A$
175 IF A$ < "A" THEN 160
180 IF A$ > "ZZZ" THEN 160
185 REM*IGNORE NONALPHABETIC STRINGS, E.G.PUNCTUATION*
190 N=N+1                   'ONE MORE WORD
200 REM*COMPUTE HASH-KEY:
210 L=L+LEN(A$)
```

```
212 A$=LEFT$(A$,16)              '16 LETTERS MAX
220 CHANGE A$ TO A               'GET LETTER-CODES
230 LET K=FNH(A(1))+1            'KEY FROM 1ST LETTER
240 REM*SEEK A$ ON OUT1:
250 SET :1,K
260 IF K>400 THEN 440            'FILE FULL!
270 READ :1, B$
280 IF B$ = " " THEN 360         'EMPTY RECORD -> NEW WORD
285 IF B$=A$ THEN 300            'FOUND IT
290 K=K+1
295 GOTO 260            'TRY NEXT RECORD
300 REM*OLD WORD FOUND AT RECORD K:
310 SET :2, K
320 READ :2,X           'COUNT OF WORD AT RECORD K
330 SET :2, K           'RE-SET FILE2 POINTER
340 PRINT :2, X+1                'ADD 1
350 GOTO 150            'NEXT INPUT WORD
360 REM*NEW WORD, NOT ON FILE:
370 W=W+1               'ANOTHER NEW WORD
380 SET :1,K, :2,K               'SET BOTH POINTERS
390 PRINT :1, A$                 'WORD A$
400 PRINT :2, 1                  'OCCURS ONCE
410 GOTO 150            'GET NEXT WORD
440 PRINT "TOO MANY WORDS!"
450 STOP
500 REM*OUTPUT:
505 PRINT
510 PRINT N;"WORDS,";W;"DIFFERENT WORDS"
515 PRINT "RATIO = ";W/N
520 PRINT
525 PRINT "MEAN LENGTH = ";L/N
530 PRINT
540 PRINT "WORDS & FREQUENCIES ON FILE"
550 PRINT "DO YOU WANT TO SEE THEM";
555 INPUT A$
560 IF A$ <> "YES" THEN 999
600 CHAIN LISTER                 'PROG TO LIST RAX FILES
999 END

READY
```

OLD HAMLET.SEQ

```
READY
LISNH 10-50
10 HAMLET
20 O, THAT THIS TOO TOO SOLID FLESH WOULD MELT,
30 THAW, AND RESOLVE ITSELF INTO A DEW !
40 OR THAT THE EVERLASTING HAD NOT FIXED
50 HIS CANON 'GAINST SELF-SLAUGHTER ! O GOD ! GOD !

READY
OLD WORDCT.XXX

READY
RUN

WORDCT.XXX   14:17          03-MAY-76

GIVE INPUT FILE.EXT PLEASE
?"HAMLET.SEQ"

262 WORDS, 162 DIFFERENT WORDS
RATIO = 0.618321

MEAN LENGTH = 4.0458

WORDS & FREQUENCIES ON FILE
DO YOU WANT TO SEE THEM ?YES

WORD          FREQUENCY
AND           6
A             7
ALL           2
AH            1
AS            1
APPETITE      1
BUT           3
BETEEM        1
BY            1
BODY          1
BEAST         1
BROTHER       1
BREAK         1
BERNARDO      1
CANON         1
COME          2
```

```
CANNOT       1
DEW          1
DE 0

TIME: 9.16 SECS.

READY
```

Notice the use of CTRL/0 in this example to halt a very long listing.

The file read by this program in the run at 14:17 (HAMLET.SEQ) is Hamlet's first soliloquy. Five lines of it (10 to 50) are listed following the program. Punctuation marks in the text have been artifically separated from the words they follow (other than commas which are separators anyway) so that they are not treated as part of those words.

The CHAIN statement is used in line 600. This statement halts the current program and brings a specified program from disc into the working-area, then runs it. In this example LISTER.BAS is called in, which prints the contents of the two files output by WORDCT.XXX. CHAIN is useful for long jobs that need to be broken into smaller segments to fit in the working-area, or which are split up for other reasons. One caution to heed when using this statement is that when one program chains another the first is lost from the working area. So beware of editing a program with a CHAIN in it, then test-running it . . . then finding it has vanished from the working area to be replaced by the chained program, not the one you were revising. In such a situation you will have to save the edited program before test-running it, or temporarily delete the CHAIN statement(s).

7.5 Exercises

(1) Write a program to list the contents of a random-access numeric file.

(2) Write a program to print the contents of a random-access string file, specified by the user, in reverse order.

(3) Write a program which takes details of a random-access file (name, type etc.) from the user, and then lists any series of records N to M on request.

(4) The example in the previous section employs a program called LISTER.BAS to list the contents of the two output files OUT1 and OUT2 produced by WORDCT.XXX, but this program is not shown. Write it.

(5) Write an improved LISTER that will print the entries on OUT1 and OUT2 according to their alphabetic order on OUT1. At present they are only partially alphabetized. (The two files must remain co-ordinated: any re-arranging of OUT1 should be matched on OUT2.)

*(6) Write a program to compute and print the average number of words per sentence, and total number of sentences, in the file HAMLET.SEQ or any file in the same format. A sentence is deemed to end when one of the strings "." or "!" or "?" is encountered.

*(7) Write a binary search program to find an entry on a sorted numeric random-access file. The binary search method, briefly, consists in looking at the mid-point of a series known to be in order, such as a vector or file, and from the value of the entry at that point deciding whether the search should proceed in the lower or upper half from there (or whether the entry is the item sought). The procedure is repeated, halving the area of search each time, until the item is found.

The following example should clarify the idea: it is the trace of a binary search - by hand - through an English dictionary of 820 pages and over 50 000 words for the word 'binary'. The mid-point was guessed roughly at each step. This does not greatly affect the number of steps taken.

STEP	PAGE	WORD FOUND	WHERE NEXT?	RANGE
1.	418	LAMA	BACK	0:418
2.	190	DEAD-ALIVE	BACK	0:190
3.	90	BRIEFCASE	BACK	0:90
4.	29	ANTIHISTAMINE	FORWARD	29:90
5.	59	BEADING	FORWARD	59:90
6.	71	BIVOUAC	BACK	59:71
7.	66	BESTRIDE	FORWARD	66:71
8.	68	BIKE	(FORWARD)	68:71
		['BINARY' is on page 68.]		

(8) Write a program that accepts an input word from the user and then reads through the sequential file HAMLET.SEQ seeking that word. Each occurence of that word on the file is printed on the terminal along with its context, the words immediately preceding and following it. The program should not abort if the word cannot be found on the file!

8. Summary

This chapter reviews some of the ground covered so far, setting it in perspective, and offers a few guidelines to the advancing programmer. Now you have the basic idea, the rest should be easy. But there is more to writing a program than knowing the grammar of a programming language.

Becoming competent in Basic requires motivation and opportunity. In this respect it is like acquiring any other skill. Programming is not an activity carried out in a vacuum: normally the programmer sets out with an objective - a task for the computer to perform. Only while one is learning is writing a program an end in itself; ordinarily it is merely a means to an end.

Trying to master Basic, without any motive for using it, is like trying to learn Russian or French just because it would be a nice educational idea, with no reason to use the language for communication. It can be done; but it requires uncommon perseverence. And the perseverence might be better expended on a less futile accomplishment.

Attempting to learn Basic without access to a conversational Basic system is also exceedingly difficult. So those with no motive or opportunity to use a Basic computer system should waste no further time in finding something more worthwhile to study.

8.1 Programming style and standards

Programs can be good or bad, efficient or inefficient, tidy or untidy - and of course they may or may not work. If you work as a programmer your employer will doubtless have a comprehensive set of standards covering every aspect of the process from drawing up a program specification to documenting the finished article, and you will have no choice but to conform to these; but even if you only write programs for yourself, the more you write, the more likely you are to want you programs to be well thought-out, and to work.

Programming is a craft. As a programmer you will want to impose, and maintain, your own standards of craftsmanship, avoiding ugly or sloppily conceived programs even if, by chance, they work. Sooner or later you will come across the phrase 'structured programming'. Loosely grouped under this general and somewhat abused slogan are several disciplines for assisting people to write clear and effective programs. An introductory text such as this cannot teach you how to write well-structured programs, but here at least are a few hints.

8.1.1 Modules

Small is beautiful. The time taken to get a program working properly increases exponentially with its length (Forsyth's second law). Therefore it makes sense to break a complex programming task into 'modules' - pieces of program each doing a relatively well defined subtask - with a clearly defined interface between them. Basic is not very richly endowed with facilities for this, but it does provide subroutines, user-defined functions and program chaining as means of fragmenting a long process; and these should be exploited to the full.

8.1.2 Working with Basic

Basic imposes certain constraints, such as the necessity of starting every line with a distinct linenumber and the limited selection of variable-names; but you can learn to live with them. In order to make the most of the resources of the language, try to work with Basic rather than fighting against it.

(1) Avoid spaghetti programs - those so littered with GOTO's that it is impossible to perceive any logical flow.

(2) Pick linenumbers and variable-names with care. Start important sections of program on hundreds or thousands. GOTO 700 and GOSUB 5000 are likely to mean more than GOTO 921 or GOSUB 71129. You are restricted to one-letter or letter-digit variable-names, but with a little imagination these can be chosen in a meaningful and systematic way.

(3) Establish your own conventions about the use of variables for loops, in subroutines, and so on; and try to stick to them.

(4) Resist the temptation to compose programs *ad lib* on the terminal. Plan them in advance. With large programs, try out a scaled-down version before embarking on the production model.

(5) Do not throw away the listing of a working program as soon as you have 'improved' it. You may need to backtrack later.

(6) Force yourself to insert REM statements when typing in a program: you will be glad of it later. And even if working for yourself, be conscientious enough to keep a listing and trial run on test data of all your

programs except the most trivial, for subsequent reference. Otherwise you may have to 're-invent the wheel' every three months or so.

(7) Eschew clever tricks which may save milliseconds of processor time or a few lines of coding but which waste many man-hours because they are so obscure. The best style is the simplest.

(8) Ensure that your algorithms work on limiting cases such as empty files or arrays with only one element, not just on ordinary run-of-the-mill data, and that they take precautions against input they cannot cope with.

There is no single way to write good programs. After all, programming is a problem-solving exercise and problem-solving demands creativity and originality. But these recommendations - which are really only common sense - should lead you in the right direction.

8.1.3 Structured program design

No doubt many people will think that the idea of structured programming in Basic is a self-contradiction. But, in fact, because Basic is so open to abuse, some knowledge of the principles of sound program design is even more necessary for the Basic programmer than for one using another language.

The essentials of structured programming (as far as the author has been able to ascertain) are: (1) to use only a small number of well-behaved control structures, normally only sequencing, repetition and selection; (2) to attempt to base the program structure on the data-structure of the problem - so that the form of the program reflects, in some sense, the form of the data; and (3) to use as far as possible natural human modes of thought, trying to impose human order on the program rather than letting the computer dictate the programmer's techniques. All these are ways of improving the chance of catching flaws at the design stage, not the checkout stage when they have already wasted time and money. The last aim usually involves what is called a 'top-down' approach - a process of successive refinement in understanding the problem/task from gross to finer levels, ultimately reaching a level low enough for computer instructions - and this in turn usually entails a modularized, hierarchical program design.

Once again the key word is 'understanding'. You cannot ask a computer a question: you can only give it an order. Therefore it cannot help you unless you understand what you want it to do.

The precepts of structured programming are worth taking to heart, but rather than attempting to translate structured programming constructs into the Basic language (which would deserve a longer book than this one) let us consider the implications for the ordinary Basic programmer.

It is important to realize that structured programming is intended as a technique for helping people get the best out of computers (not the other way round), and not to get distracted from the real issues. Some of the modern mythology surrounding the vogue for structured programming verges on the mystical, and can be downright confusing. It could be summed up as 'Zen and the Art of Computer Programming'. If there is one point which does emerge from the heated structured-programming debate it is this: no one can write an effective program without understanding clearly what the computer is to do. So thorough problem-analysis is the most vital part of computer programming.

Finally, do not lose sight of the fact that the ultimate aim of writing a program is to get some results that help solve a problem not to produce an elegant program.

8.2 Error detection and correction

This is called 'debugging' in the trade. Again it is a skill, not an exact science. As you gain (bitter) experience you will learn more about the sort of mistakes that you and the computer, in conjunction, can make. One fact you must be prepared to accept is: if it's interesting, it won't work - not at first, anyway (Forsyth's first law).

Three different kinds of errors can arise in a Basic program: (1) syntax errors; (2) execution errors; and (3) logical errors.

8.2.1 Syntax errors

These errors occur when your program violates the rules of the Basic language. When an attempt is made to run a program containing such errors, the Basic interpreter rejects it and informs the user which lines are incorrect. It is never actually executed. These errors are normally the easiest to deal with. In many cases they arise out of simple spelling mistakes, missing commas and so forth. (Some Basic systems detect syntax errors when the line is typed in.)

8.2.2 Execution errors

Execution errors happen when a running program attempts something illogical or impossible, although it is syntactically valid. Typical examples are dividing by zero and trying to access an array-element outside the bounds set for the array. The former is not 'fatal' (Basic prints an OVERFLOW warning but carries on using the largest number 1.7E38 as the result), while the latter is fatal (Basic prints an error-message and halts the program). Generally runtime error-messages are quite informative; but just because a program, say, runs OUT OF DATA IN LINE 650 it does not mean that line 650 is wrong: more probably another line in the program (e.g. a DATA statement) needs attention. So although Basic tells you where it found an error, you may need to track down the source of that error elsewhere.

8.2.3 Logical errors

Logical errors are those which do not cause a program to fail, but which cause it to produce the wrong answers. These are the most troublesome. Unfortunately there is nothing to guarantee that a program consisting entirely of valid Basic statements which runs successfully to completion is actually giving the right results. There are three stages in getting rid of a logical error: firstly detecting the existence of an error; secondly finding where it is; and thirdly putting it right. None of these need be very simple. In this sort of error-correction, intuition (methodically applied) plays an important role.

8.2.4 Debugging

Often a few extra PRINT statements, showing the values of key variables at critical points, will shed light on the murkiest programming problem. But do not rush headlong into a program, changing lines haphazardly, and confusing the situation still further. Above all, avoid 'thinking on-line': if you cannot spot the source of the trouble at once, go away and think about it unhurriedly.

The art of debugging lies in forcing the program to reveal its behaviour patterns - what variables are being changed, what variables are not being changed, which paths are being selected, which paths are not selected, and so on. Some Basic systems have an immediate mode so that a statement typed without a linenumber preceding it will be executed immediately. Thus, for example,

```
PRINT A, (B+X)/2
```

would output the current values of the variable A and the expression (B+X)/2. This can be extremely revealing just after an unexplained error condition has aborted a program. Other systems provide sophisticated debugging tools which let the user trace program execution and/or set break-points at which the program is halted and variables can be examined or changed before proceeding. However, these debugging aids may themselves require considerable learning effort, and of course no such assistance may be available on your computer; so it is wise to know how to proceed without them.

As a general rule, if the error is complex enough to puzzle the program's author, it will also puzzle the computer: so you must be prepared for error-diagnostics which are misleading - at least to your way of thinking. You must also be ready to go back to the drawing board and re-examine all your tacit assumptions. Then return to the terminal only when you know what information you want about the program's behaviour: what variable values are critical and which, when you are able to monitor their changing status by means of inserted PRINT statements, will reduce the number of alternative possible explanations of the program's misbehaviour. In short, you must approach the incorrect program with a hypothesis, or else you will not know what to look for. This is why a leisurely re-think, away from the terminal, is usually necessary.

Faults can occur in so many ways that there is no general remedy. Learning to locate them is, oddly enough, part of the fun (and programming can be fun). As suggested above, the programmer's attitude is more important than any rules of thumb. Perhaps the best attitude might be called 'defensive programming', on the basis that prevention is better than cure. Try to anticipate errors and eradicate them at the design stage by adopting rigorous standards, by checking your input, by running test cases, and so on. In the last resort, if completely bogged down, start again from scratch and do it a different way: some programs are ill-fated and just have to be scrapped. It is worth remembering in this context that the computer will do anything you instruct it to do - even if it is stupid.

8.3 Where do we go from here?

Where indeed?

Having learned something about computing, you may want to go deeper into the subject. Three possibilities are: (1) learning more about Basic; (2) learning another high-level programming language such as Algol-60, Algol-68, APL, Cobol, Fortran, Lisp, Pascal, PL/1, POP-2, Simula or Snobol, to name only a few, or a low-level assembly language; (3) learning more about computing in general, either about commercial data-processing in the real world or about scientific applications.

This subsection selects just three useful books that may interest the advancing programmer. There are of course many more.

Those wishing to pursue Basic further will find that the best book on the subject is *Basic Programming* by John Kemeney and Thomas Kurtz:

second edition, Wiley (1971) which was written by the authors of the language. It is recommended to anyone intending to do a lot of Basic programming: it uses a version of Basic very similar to the one described here, and is full of instructive examples.

A very helpful book for all who realize that programming is one branch of problem-solving in general is *How to Solve It* by G. Polya: second edition, Princeton University Press (1957). This is a guide to 'heuristic', the art of solving problems; and although most of the examples are algebraic or geometrical, it can be recommended even to the non-mathematical reader as of general interest.

Also very informative is *A Practical Approach to Computing* by Arms, Baker and Pengelly: Wiley (1976).

8.4 Other versions of Basic

The user transferring between machines will find, as mentioned earlier, that Basic is not fully compatible on different computers. The nucleus of the language is the same, but the extended facilities differ. Every manufacturer's handbook tries to convince the reader that their peculiar 'enhanced' Basic is the greatest thing since sliced bread; but all too often you end up longing for a good old-fashioned unsliced loaf.

This section describes the most common variations in the Basic language, compared with the version used in this book. None of the lists are exhaustive, but they cover the main points of variation.

8.4.1 Restrictions

Some features of DEC10 Basic are commonly unavailable on other systems.

The LET keyword may not be optional.
Blank lines and in-line comments may be forbidden.
Maximum length of string variables may need to be specified in the program, and may be less than 132 characters.
String vectors may not be permitted.
Predefined string functions (such as MID$) may not be provided.
Double-quotes may be mandatory for all string constants.
The <PA> delimiter may not be usable in PRINT lists.
Semicolons may be compulsory between text constants and numeric items (where the DEC10 version assumes them if omitted) in PRINT.
Random-access files may be absent.
Run-time allocation of a file to a channel (FILE) may not be possible.

Files may have to exist (with a fixed size) before a program can use them - i.e. a program may not be able to make a new file, or extend an old one.

Multiple line function definitions may be illegal.

8.4.2 Extra facilities

Some limitations of DEC10 Basic may be lifted.

An integer data-type may be available.

A subroutine mechanism (CALL) for genuine subroutines with local variables and arguments may be implemented, as well as GOSUB.

A common core-store area (COM) may be available for passing data between CHAINed programs.

Multi-line statements and/or multi-statement lines may be allowed.

Logical connectives (NOT, AND and OR) may be permitted in IF conditions; and IF-THEN-ELSE may be allowed too.

There may be a line-input statement for reading a whole line of input as a string - including spaces, commas, quotation marks etc.

MAT READ and MAT PRINT may be possible on files.

String matrices and 3D numeric arrays may be allowed.

Functions which take string arguments and which yield string results may be definable.

8.4.3 Differences

Some things are just done in different ways.

Substring selection may be done in some other way.

Arrays may be numbered from 1 not 0.

ASCII character code may not be used.

MAT INPUT may function differently.

Maximum and minimum numeric values (overflow and underflow) may well differ, as may the precision to which numbers are represented.

The RND and TIM functions may need arguments, which may have some significance; and the set of predefined functions may vary from machine to machine.

The largest possible line-number and the longest possible program will almost certainly differ.

8.4.4 Machine-independent Basic

If you know that you may need to swap computers at some stage, it may be worth-while trying as far as practicable to write machine-independent Basic programs. To some extent, naturally, this will mean foregoing some powerful local features; but it may have compensating advantages.

Here are some suggestions.

Stick to the materials from the first four chapters of this book (excluding PRINT USING with string fields), plus simple assignment, comparison and input-output of strings.
Cut out in-line comments after the apostrophe.
Use only numeric functions.
Avoid multi-line function definitions; and stick to one statement per line.
Avoid all file-access!
Use special local enhancements (marked by REM statements) only at your own risk.

This may sound like a recipe for dull programs. It is; but writing dull programs can be surprisingly interesting.

8.5 Example program

Our final example (SYNTAX.XXX) is chosen to counteract the prevalent notion that all computing is (1) numerical; (2) analytic, and (3) deadly serious. It is a program that uses a simplified English grammar to construct sentences, thus producing short literary compositions ('poems' would be too dignified a description). It is very definitely (1) linguistic; (2) synthetic; and (3) frivolous. It is synthetic in the sense that it produces large amounts of new output from a few prescriptive rules rather than attempting to reduce a vast amount of input data to a few descriptive rules by analysis.

The program makes use of what is known in linguistics as a 'generative grammar'. This allows considerably more flexibility of sentence-forms than the most common method employed in computer poetry, which can be described as 'slotting'. Slotting involves selecting one of a limited number of incomplete sentence-frames and simply filling in the gaps in the framework with appropriate parts of speech. A generative grammar, on the other hand, permits a theoretically infinite number of sentence forms.

A very simple generative grammar appears below. It is capable of producing gems like 'the old postman lovingly bites each dog' and 'one ugly dog chases the fiercely beautiful postman'. It consists of an ordered set of re-writing rules, specifying that a sentence can be re-written as a noun-phrase followed by a verb-phrase; that a noun-phrase can be further expanded into an article, an optional adjectival phrase and then a noun; that a verb-phrase can be expanded into an optional adverb, a verb, then a noun-phrase; and so on down the hierarchy to the level of particular word-classes.

1. S => NP + VP.
2. NP => Art + (AP) + Noun.
3. VP => (Adv) + Verb + NP.
4. AP => (Adv) + Adj + (AP).
5. Art => the/each/one . . .
6. Noun => postman/dog . . .
7. Verb => bites/chases/kicks . . .
8. Adv => fiercely/lovingly . . .
9. Adj => old/ugly/beautiful . . .

Rules of this sort can be incorporated into a program as subroutines. In fact the program would be impossible without subroutines, since its underlying principle is that a grammatical rule is embodied as a subroutine. The random-number generator RND comes into play both for picking particular words from a class and for making choices between alternative paths where the rules allow more than one branch.

As illustration, flowcharts for the sentence-generating section (lines 500 to 800 in the program) and for the noun-phrase routine (lines 2000 to 2250) are shown below. The small circles represent choice-points where the RND function is used to decide which of two alternative paths to follow. The routine PICK selects and prints a word of a given type (e.g. PICK Noun). In the program the word-selection routine begins at line 1000 and uses T to indicate the word-type required. Thus immediately before each GOSUB 1000 there is a LET statement assigning a value between 1 and 10 to the variable T.

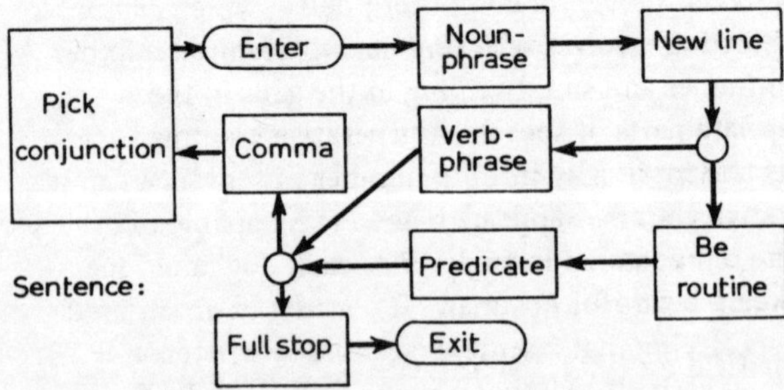

Fig. 8. Sentence routine.

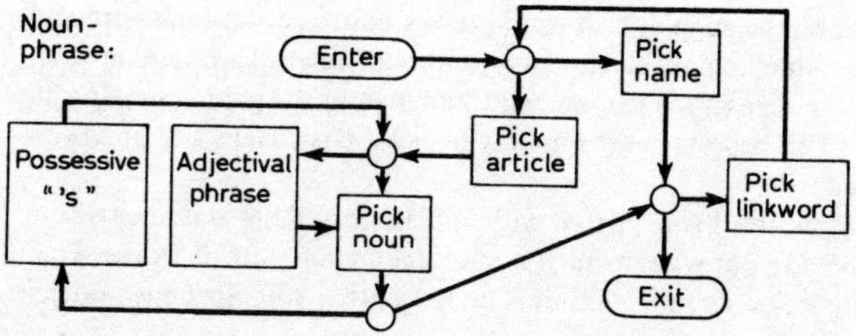

Fig. 9. Noun phrase routine.

The ten word-types are as follows.

Type	Name	Example
1.	Auxiliary	WILL
2.	Noun	LOVE
3.	Transitive verb	DESTROY
4.	Adjective	BEAUTIFUL
5.	Adverb	AMAZINGLY
6.	Name	EROS
7.	Linkword	OF
8.	Conjunction	AND
9.	Intransitive Verb	SLEEP
10.	Article	THE

The category linkword comprises prepositions, transitive verb participles and a variety of linking phrases. The words themselves can be seen in the DATA statements after line 5000. Most were culled from an anonymous Elizabethan lyric.

The main subroutines in the program are listed below.

First Line	Routine
1000	Pick and print a word of given type (T)
2000	Construct a noun-phrase
2500	Construct an adjectivel phrase
3000	Construct a verb-phrase
3500	Construct a phrase using 'to be'
4000	Form a predicate for the verb 'to be'
4500	Make up a title

Some of the grammatical routines, for instance the noun-phrase routine, employ the device of optionally looping back to their beginning. Thus a noun-phrase can be simple, or it can have the construction Linkword and noun-phrase added on at the end any number of times. Examples are: ‘the man’; ‘the man in the garden’; and ‘the man in the garden looking at the flower’. This process is used mainly because Basic lacks any provision for recursion.

The program itself is peppered with explanatory REM statements to help you thread your way through it, and understand how it works. The central sentence-generating section is on lines 500–800. Specimen output is printed after the program listing.

```
LIS

SYNTAX.XXX    11:40                30-APR-76
1 REM*SENTENCE GENERATOR:
10 DEF FNN(A)=INT(RND*A+1)
20 DIM W(10), W$(250)
100 REM**READ WORDS FROM DATA:
110 LET W(0)=K=0
112 FOR I=1 TO 10                  '10 WORD-TYPES
115     READ X$
120     IF X$="***" THEN 150               'END MARKER
122     K=K+1
125     W$(K)=X$
130     GOTO 115
150     W(I)=K             'PLACE OF LAST I-TYPE WORD IN W$
155 NEXT I
200         PRINT "HOW MANY COMPOSITIONS";
210 INPUT K
220 FOR C= 1 TO K
222     RANDOMIZE
225     PRINT
228     PRINT
230     PRINT TAB(8); "COMPOSITION ENTITLED:"
240     PRINT TAB(7);
250     GOSUB 4500        'TITLE ROUTINE
260     PRINT
270     PRINT
280     LET N=FNN(8)+FNN(8)
290     LET N9=FNN(8)
300     FOR S=1 TO N
```

```
500       REM**SENTENCE:
510     GOSUB 2000        'NOUN-PHRASE
515     PRINT
516     PRINT TAB(2);
520     IF RND>.4 THEN 600      'USE BE-ROUTINE
530     GOSUB 3000        'VERB-PHRASE
550     GOTO 700          'END SENTENCE
600     GOSUB 3500        'BE-ROUTINE
610     GOSUB 4000        'PREDICATE
700     REM*ENDING:
710     IF RND>.125 THEN 800          'FULLSTOP
720     PRINT  ","
730     T=8               'CONJUNCTION
740     GOSUB 1000        'WORD SELECTOR
750     GOTO 500          'REPEAT
800     PRINT "."
810     IF S<>N9 THEN 830
820     PRINT
830     NEXT S            'NEXT SENTENCE
840     PRINT             'NEWLINE
850 NEXT C                'NEXT COMPOSITION
860 PRINT
870 PRINT TAB(8); "COPYRIGHT, GRIBBLY'S POETRY WORKSHOP."
880 STOP
1000      REM**WORD-SELECTOR (T=TYPE):
1001 N0=W(T-1)            'LAST WORD IN W$ BEFORE TYPE T
1005 I=FNN(W(T)-N0)  .
1010 PRINT " ";W$(N0+I);
1020 RETURN
2000      REM**NOUN-PHRASE:
2010 IF RND>.2 THEN 2050      'USE NOUN
2020 T=6                  'NAME
2030 GOSUB 1000
2040 GOTO 2200            'ENDING
2050 REM*USING NOUN
2055 T=10                 'ARTICLE
2060 GOSUB 1000
2070 IF RND>.25 THEN 2090
2080 GOSUB 2500           'ADJ-PHRASE
2090 T=2                  'NOUN
```

```
2100 GOSUB 1000
2110 IF RND>.1 THEN 2150
2120 PRINT " 'S";          'POSSESSIVE
2130 GOTO 2070
2150 REM*ENDING:
2200 IF RND>.125 THEN 2250
2220 T=7                   'LINKWORD
2230 GOSUB 1000
2240 GOTO 2000             'REPEAT
2250 RETURN                'END OF NOUN-PHRASE
2500       REM**ADJECTIVAL PHRASE:
2510 IF RND>.2 THEN 2540
2520 T=5                   'ADVERB
2530 GOSUB 1000
2540 T=4                   'ADJECTIVE
2550 GOSUB 1000
2560 IF RND>.1 THEN 2600                    'FINISH
2570 IF RND>.333 THEN 2510                  'REPEAT
2580 PRINT " AND";
2590 GOTO 2510             'REPEAT
2600 RETURN                'END OF ADJ-PHRASE
3000       REM**VERB-PHRASE:
3010 T1=INT(RND+.5)              'TRANSITIVE OR NOT
3020 A1=INT(RND+.5)              'AUXILIARY OR NOT
3030 IF A1<1 THEN 3070
3040 T=1                   'AUX
3050 GOSUB 1000
3060 GOSUB 3300            'NOT (OR NOT!)
3070 T=3                   'T-VERB
3080 IF T1>0 THEN 3100          'TRANSITIVE?
3090 T=9                   'I-VERB
3100 GOSUB 1000            'PICK MAIN VERB
3110 IF A1>0 THEN 3130          'NO S IF AUX USED
3120 PRINT "S"; 'VERBAL SUFFIX
3130 IF T1<1 THEN 3150          'NO OBJECT IF INTRANSITIVE
3140 GOSUB 2000            'NOUN-PHRASE
3150 RETURN                'END OF VERB-PHRASE
3300       REM**NOT/ADV SUBROUTINE:
3310 IF RND>.1 THEN 3330
3320 PRINT " NOT";
3330 IF RND>.125 THEN 3360
```

```
3340 T=5                     'ADVERB
3350 GOSUB 1000
3360 RETURN                  'END OF NOT/ADV ROUTINE
3500       REM**TO BE OR NOT TO BE:
3510 IF RND>.4 THEN 3560                'USE IS/WAS
3520 T=1                     'USE AUX
3530 GOSUB 1000
3540 GOSUB 3300              'NOT/ADV ROUTINE
3550 PRINT " BE";
3555 RETURN
3560 X$=" IS"
3570 IF RND>.333 THEN 3590              'PICK BE-WORD
3580 X$=" WAS"
3590 PRINT X$;
3600 GOSUB 3300              'NOT/ADV ROUTINE
3610 RETURN                  'END OF BEING
4000       REM**PREDICATE (3 TYPES):
4010 ON FNN(3) GOTO 4020,4040,4060
4020 T=7                     'LINKWORD
4030 GOSUB 1000
4040 GOSUB 2000              'NOUN-PHRASE
4050 RETURN
4060 GOSUB 2500              'ADJ-PHRASE
4070 RETURN                  'END OF PRED
4500       REM**TITLE:
4510 ON FNN(4) GOTO 4520,4540,4560,4580
4520 GOSUB 2000              'NOUN-PHRASE
4530 RETURN
4540 GOSUB 2500              'ADJ-PHRASE
4550 RETURN
4560 GOSUB 4000              'PRED
4570 RETURN
4580 PRINT " TO";
4590 T=3                     'T-VERB
4600 GOSUB 1000
4610 GOSUB 2000              'OBJECT OF VERB
4620 RETURN
5000       REM**DATAWORDS (TYPES 1-10):
5100 DATA WILL,MAY,MUST,DID,CAN,SHOULD,WOULD
5110 DATA COULD,MIGHT,CANNOT,SMALL
5199 DATA "***"
```

```
5200 DATA DESPAIR,HOPE,LOVER,OCEAN,FIRE,SPIRIT,WORD
5210 DATA IDEA,SMILE,FLOWER,LADY,ROSE,FLAME,HEART
5220 DATA FANCY,SUMMER,WINTER,HOUR,DAY,BIRTH,EARTH
5230 DATA SEED,GARDEN,EYE,YEAR,TIME,WORTH,SERVICE,LOVE
5240 DATA DELIGHT,STAR,SKY,FRIEND,END,FROWN,LOOK,SMILE
5250 DATA MAN,WOMAN,CHILD,BODY,FEAR,HAND,CRIME,WORLD
5299 DATA "***"
5300 DATA DESTROY,LOVE,NEED,WANT,HURT,STRIKE,FORM
5310 DATA FEEL,FEAR,LOVE,MAKE,UNMAKE,KNOW,PROVE,SEE
5399 DATA "***"
5400 DATA BEAUTIFUL,CRUEL,AMAZING,LOVELY,CUNNING
5410 DATA FALSE,TRUE,GAUDY,COLD,DEAD,DARK,WARM,YOUNG
5420 DATA MORTAL,CHOSEN,BRIGHT,ENDLESS,OLD,COMING,LOVING
5430 DATA DIVINE,UNWORTHY,BEST,BLESSED,HUMBLE,STILL,HIGH
5440 DATA FAIR,SWEET,SMILING,CHEERFUL,PERFECT,NAKED,GENTLE,HIDDEN
5499 DATA "***"
5500 DATA AMAZINGLY,SOMEHOW,REALLY,INEXPLICABLY
5510 DATA GAILY,FIERCELY,SUDDENLY,STRANGELY,CARELESSLY
5520 DATA UTTERLY,WILLINGLY,GRADUALLY,ENDLESSLY,BEAUTIFULLY
5530 DATA GREATLY,ONLY,STILL,NEVER,ALWAYS,PERFECTLY
5599 DATA "***"
5600 DATA EROS,VENUS,"MY LADY",NATURE,PARADISE,TIME,VIRTUE,HOPE
5610 DATA MINE,IT,LOVE,RICHARD,MEI-LYNN,EVERYTHING,DESPAIR
5620 DATA "NO ONE",SOMEONE,NOTHING,EVERYBODY,OURS,YOURS
5699 DATA "***"
5700 DATA OF,IN,FROM,WITH,OF,NEAR,BEYOND,WITHOUT
5710 DATA LIKE,HAVING,LOVING,WITHIN,REACHING,ABOVE
5720 DATA "LOOKING AT",UPON,ON,FROM,AS,BEHIND,AGAINST,"IN LOVE WITH"
```

```
5799 DATA "***"
5800 DATA AND,BUT,BECAUSE,SO,ALTHOUGH,YET,"AND YET",
                                          THEREFORE,IF
5810 DATA WHILE,WHEN,WHEREAS,FOR,"SO THAT","AND SO",
                                            "AND EVEN"
5899 DATA "***"
5900 DATA SLEEP,FALL,DIE,REMAIN,CHANGE,SING,EXPLORE,
                                            BLOW,THINK
5910 DATA GROW,SPEAK,FADE,EXIST,FLEE,COME,EXCEL,HOPE,
                                                  LOOK
5920 DATA FROWN,SMILE,THINK,LOVE,FAIL,WHISPER,
                                      SURRENDER
5999 DATA "***"
6000 DATA THE,EACH,NO,EVERY,SOME,MY,YOUR,THIS,THE
6010 DATA ITS,HIS,HER,OUR,ONE,THAT,ANY,ANOTHER,
                                        "EVEN THE"
6020 DATA "THE ONLY","ONLY THE","AN OLD","A SMALL",
                                       "SOME OF THE"
6099 DATA "***"
9999 END

READY
RUN

SYNTAX.XXX    11:53          30-APR-76

HOW MANY COMPOSITIONS ?2

      COMPOSITION ENTITLED:
      CHEERFUL

MY SMILE
  IS LOOKING AT YOUR FLAME.
HIS WOMAN
  IS NO CHILD.
RICHARD
  IS LOOKING AT ITS FROWN.
EVERY YOUNG ROSE
  SHALL ONLY BE SOME SERVICE

      COMPOSITION ENTITLED:
      OUR SMILE

THAT YEAR
  MIGHT CARELESSLY BE HAVING MY HIGH YEAR.
```

DESPAIR
  WILL LOVE PARADISE.

AN OLD SUMMER
  IS MY HAND,
WHEREAS AN OLD STILL BEAUTIFUL FRIEND AS ANOTHER YEAR
  SHALL BE ON YOUR WINTER,
WHEN A SMALL SPIRIT
  FORMS VIRTUE.
EVERYTHING
  SHALL BE GENTLE.
ANOTHER PERFECT FIRE
  FEELS TIME REACHING ANOTHER END.
AN OLD HAND
  IS EVEN THE GRADUALLY DARK GARDEN.
MEI-LYNN
  CAN NOT FAIL.
A SMALL WORTH
  DID BE YOURS.
THE FROWN
  WOULD BE HAVING PARADISE,
SO YOUR DARK HEART
  KNOWS ANY IDEA.
THE FROWN
  FEARS DESPAIR FROM AN OLD SMILE.
EVERY FLOWER
  IS IN LOVE WITH EVEN THE SWEET AND DIVINE FROWN.

COPYRIGHT, GRIBBLY'S POETRY WORKSHOP.

TIME: 1.28 SECS.

Although the grammar is restricted to indicative sentences using singular nouns and the total vocabulary is under 250 words, some of the sentences produced by this program have a certain aphoristic poignancy, and readers have suggested that with a little human editing the compositions could be quite good.

Nevertheless the compositions fail to hang together as wholes. In effect the computer is churning out grammatical nonsense. Unrelated sentences are juxtaposed at random. Any semblance of connectedness arises because they draw on a restricted and deliberately vague vocabulary.

The burden of making sense of these sentences is placed firmly on the human reader. Shifting this burden on to the computer, where it belongs, is the real problem, and any progress in this direction would be a significant conceptual advance in the quest for genuine computer poetry.

Having admitted the limitations of the program, it is fair to state that watching the machine churn out novel compositions tirelessly at 30 characters per second can be quite impressive. The number of possible constructions is limited only by the periodicity of the random-number generator; and with a good random-number generator, such as the Basic RND function, the chances of repeating a sentence, let alone a complete composition, are very remote.

8.6 Projects

You are now on your own. There is no real need for any more programming exercises. It is time to apply what you have learned to your own problems. However some of the suggestions below might be worth tackling if they appeal to you and if you have time.

(1) Improve SYNTAX.XXX by increasing its vocabulary to at least 500 words; by removing the DATA statements and placing the words on a sequential file to be read at the beginning of the program; by extending the grammar to produce questions (in the form Aux + NOUN-PHRASE + I-verb + (Adverb) ? or Aux + NOUN-PHRASE + T-verb + NOUN-PHRASE ?) and eventually also imperatives (in the form I-verb! or T-verb + NOUN-PHRASE!); and by adding a new category of 'word' (type 11) which consists of exclamations and complete sentences such as "GOOD LORD!" and "THE MIND BOGGLES!" to be inserted as titles or as sentences occasionally. Also try 'tuning' the grammar by experimenting with different probabilities for various constructions.

(2) Write an automatic sentence-generating program which uses semantic information to produce coherent connected sentences. (This is a long-term project.) One approach is to collect words into semantic groupings; another is to store a list of attributes for each word, expressing its relations with other words and its permissible roles in sentences. No one has so far been very successful at this.

(3) Design and implement a suite of banking programs which maintain a file of all your cheques (debits) and earnings (credits) for 12 months including the last month - discarding records over one year old when the data for the current month is added - and which produces monthly statements. The statement should not only show the latest balance but

also the projected balance for 3, 6 and 12 months ahead based on past trends. Mail the output to your bank manager when he sends you his computerized bank statement. If the two differ, and the difference is not in your favour, attach a rude note.

(4) Plan a pattern-recognition program which will recognize an input handwritten character as a letter A to Z or a digit 0 to 9. Assume that an optical scanner reads a handprinted character and translates it into a 32 by 32 matrix, each element of which is 1 (dark) or 0 (blank). Each row of this matrix can be coded as a binary 32-bit number. The input device encodes the matrix as a series of 32 32-bit binary numbers, each of which represents one line of the matrix. Your program should be able to read these 32 lines and decide what character was read by the optical scanner. (It is probably best to devise a program that can learn to improve its performance as a result of feedback.)

(5) Explore the possibilities of computer art. Although some thinkers consider this a field doomed to sterility (and no one has convincingly refuted them yet), there are a number of interesting technical problems to be attacked in the attempt to achieve good computer-generated art. Use whatever output devices (such as plotters) are available at your installation. Some interesting patterns can be displayed on an ordinary teleprinter if you cannot get hold of any special graphic device.

(6) Design and specify your ideal programming language, drawing on the concepts you have learned and where possible improving on them. Utlimately you should be able to implement it on an existing computer.

(7) Write a problem that does something useful, and works.

(8) Repeat the previous exercise until you are tired.

Good luck! And enjoy it.

Appendices & Answers

Appendix A. ASCII character set

The printable ASCII characters are given below along with their decimal codes. This output was produced by a Basic program.

CCODES.XXX   12:01   20-MAY-76

CODE/CHARACTER		CODE/CHARACTER	
32		59	;
33	!	60	<
34	"	61	=
35	#	62	>
36	$	63	?
37	%	64	@
38	&	65	A
39	'	66	B
40	(	67	C
41	)	68	D
42	*	69	E
43	+	70	F
44	,	71	G
45	-	72	H
46	.	73	I
47	/	74	J
48	0	75	K
49	1	76	L
50	2	77	M
51	3	78	N
52	4	79	O
53	5	80	P
54	6	81	Q
55	7	82	R
56	8	83	S
57	9	84	T
58	:	85	U

CODE/CHARACTER		CODE/CHARACTER	
86	V	91	[
87	W	92	\
88	X	93	]
89	Y	94	^
90	Z	95	—

TIME: 0.38 SECS.

Lower case letters a to z are represented by ASCII codes 97 to 122, but most terminals are only equipped for capitals.

Basic users may find that code-numbers below 32 are not usable. The number 32 represents a blank space. Your computer may have a different character code. In almost all coding schemes A<B<C . . . <Z and 0<1<2 . . . <9 as characters. The IBM EBCDIC code is very widespread. If you intend doing much character manipulation, you will need to find out the code used on your machine.

Appendix B. List of Basic statements

This appendix describes all Basic statements except those for file-handling (see Appendix D) and matrix-manipulation (see Appendix E).

In the schematic statement-patterns, words in capitals are part of the Basic statements themselves (e.g. INPUT) and would appear as they stand in a Basic program. Words in lower case letters describe parts which are replaced in use by particular instances. Thus where 'formula' occurs it would be replaced by a formula, such as (A+B)^2, to form a valid Basic statement.

The terms used include 'var' which stands for any variable-name, and 'formula' which stands for any valid Basic expression, string or numeric. Unless otherwise specified, 'var' may also designate an array-element. If a variable or formula must be string or numeric it is qualified by having 'string-' or 'numeric-' prefixed; if there is no prefix, either type may be used.

Portions enclosed in square brackets are optional, and parts followed immediately by an asterisk may be repeated any number of times. Thus

```
line READ var [, var]*
```

can be replaced by any of the following.

```
100 READ X
200 READ X, Y
234 READ X,Y,G(I+10)
```

All Basic statements must be preceded by a linenumber in the range 0 to 99999. Spaces are not significant in Basic statements, except within string constants.

line CHAIN string-formula [,numeric-formula]
Halts the current program and starts executing the saved program named in the string-formula at the linenumber nearest to the value of the numeric-formula, or at the first line if none is given.

line CHANGE string-formula TO vector
Converts the string to a series of ASCII decimal codes which are put into the vector. Element 0 of the vector receives the number of characters in the string (N) and elements 1 to N receive the codes for those characters.

line CHANGE vector TO string-var
Reverses the above: element 0 of the vector should indicate the number of characters for transfer (N), and elements 1 to N are treated as ASCII codes whose corresponding characters are put into the receiving string.

line DATA item [,item]*
The items are numeric or string constants, separated from each other by commas. Strings may be enclosed in quotes, and must be in quotes if they contain commas or tabs or spaces or start with a non-alphabetic character. READ statements extract data-items one by one from DATA statements in the program, starting with the first item and continuing sequentially.

line DEF FNz [(argument [,argument]*)] = formula
Defines a new function. Its name must be three letters, the first two being FN; the third is shown here as z but can be any letter. The arguments are named like numeric variables but serve as place-holders local to the function definition, to be replaced by the values of the expressions in the corresponding positions when the function is used. The formula defines the function, employing the arguments, if any, to refer to the values that will replace them when the function is evaluated.

If a function is defined by a sequence of Basic instructions not in terms of an arithmetic expression then the equal sign and the formula to its right are omitted, and the function definition is ended by FNEND. Somewhere in a multi-line function definition the function-name should be given a value (see Section 5.3.1).

line DIM[ENSION] name(size) [,name(size)]*

This statement declares one or more array-names and their sizes. An array-name may be a letter or a letter followed by a digit. The size indicates its maximum subscript value. Arrays may have one or two dimensions: the size is one numeric constant for one-dimensional arrays, or two numbers separated by a comma for two-dimensional arrays. (Variables and expressions may not be used to declare an array's size. An array may not be dimensioned by DIM more than once in one program.)

Array-elements are numbered from 0 not 1; and the default upper bound for arrays not mentioned in a DIM statement is 10.

line END

Informs the compiler that there are no more program statements. It must be the last statement of every program and may not appear elsewhere. (To halt a program elsewhere, use STOP.)

line FNEND

Terminates a multi-line function definition, and acts as a return point when the function is executed.

line FOR var = firstvalue TO lastvalue [STEP stepsize]

Opens a loop controlled by a counter. The numeric formula first value is first evaluated and assigned to the variable (the 'index'). Then the instructions up to the NEXT with the same index are executed (provided that the index-variable is not initially greater than the value of the numeric expression last value). Then the index is incremented by the value of the expression after STEP (or +1 if this part is not present) and control returns to the statement just after the FOR, unless the index has exceeded the last value in which case the program continues with the statement after NEXT.

STEP may be replaced by the word BY, and if the optional stepsize is negative looping continues till the index is less than the last value (otherwise until it is greater). First value, last value and stepsize are all numeric formulas (see also NEXT).

line GOSUB linenumber

Transfers execution to the statement with the second linenumber. Execution then continues normally until a RETURN is reached, when control returns to the statement just after the GOSUB.

line GOTO linenumber

Branches to the second linenumber and continues execution from there.

line IF formula relation formula [,]THEN linenumber

If the relation holds between the two formulas, control passes to the statement with the second linenumber; otherwise it continues with the next statement in sequence. THEN may be replaced by the word GOTO. When comparing strings a rank order is determined according to their ASCII codes. (The relation symbols are described in Chapter 2.)

line INPUT var [,var]*

The program pauses and the computer prints a question-mark. The user responds by typing in a constant for each variable (or array element) in the input list - numbers for numeric variables and string constants for string variables. If more than one constant is to be typed in, each is separated from its neighbour by a comma. Strings need not be in quotes as long as they do not contain separators such as commas or blanks or start with a non-alphabetic character. The values typed by the user are given, in order, to the variables in the input list.

line [LET] var = [var =]* formula

Assigns the value of the formula (or expression) on the right to the variable(s) (or array-element(s)) on the left. Arithmetic expressions normally take the form Item Operator Item where the items are numbers, variables, array-elements, function references or complete sub-expressions (which may be in brackets). The operators are discussed in Chapter 2.

Numeric variables must be given numeric values, and string variables must be given string values.

line MARGIN numeric-formula

Sets the right-hand margin of the terminal to the position specified by the numeric formula, which must not exceed 132.

line NEXT var

Marks the end of the FOR loop with the matching variable (the 'index'). Each FOR must have one subsequent NEXT. When FOR loops are nested the inner loop or loops must be completely enclosed: they may not overlap. On normal exit from a FOR loop via NEXT the index-variable has the last value it took before exceeding the terminal value specified after TO in the FOR statement.

line NOPAGE
Cancels a previous PAGE statement: terminal output is no longer divided into pages. NOPAGE is the default mode.

line NOQUOTE
Cancels the effect of QUOTE: terminal output is no longer in 'quote' mode. NOQUOTE is the default mode.

line ON numeric-formula [,] GOTO linenumber [,linenumber]*
Control passes to the Nth linenumber after the GOTO where N is the value of the numeric formula. If N is less than 1 or greater than the number of linenumbers after the GOTO, an error results.

line PAGE numeric-formula
Causes subsequent teletype output to be divided automatically into pages of N lines each, where N is the value of the numeric formula.

line PRINT [item [separator item]* [separator]]
Prints values on the terminal. The items are string or numeric formulas (or TAB(N) which causes the printer to move to position N unless it has already been passed in which case nothing happens). The separators are commas for normal wide spacing or semicolons for compressed spacing. The formulas are evaluated and their values are printed on the terminal in the order in which they appear in the output list, with spacing dependent on the separators between them.

A PRINT with no following output list causes one blank line to be printed. Ending a PRINT statement with a separator suppresses the final carriage-return and line-feed.

line PRINT USING image, formula [, formula]*
Prints the formula(s) according to layout specified in the 'image'. An image may be a string-formula or a linenumber. If it is a string the output format is governed by the contents of that string. If it is a linenumber, output format is governed by the characters on the line referred to, which should consist of a linenumber, a colon and then the format-control characters (see Chapter 4).

line QUOTE
After this statement all strings for terminal output are printed within quotes if they contain commas or spaces or tabs or begin with a non-alphabetic character, until the next NOQUOTE statement.

line RANDOM[IZE]
Causes the predefined function RND to start generating a new series of random numbers.

line READ var [, var]*
Extracts data from DATA statements and puts them into one or more variables or array-elements. String constants must be read into string variables and numeric constants into numeric variables. Each READ starts reading from the point where the previous one left off, or, with the first READ in a program, at the first item in the first DATA statement (see also RESTORE).

line REM comment
Starts a line of non-executable comment, which can be any printable text. If execution is sent to a REM statement it has no effect and control passes on to the next executable statement.

Remarks may also be added to any line except an image line or DATA by typing an apostrophe after the statement: all characters between the apostrophe and the end of the line are then commentary.

line RESTORE [sign]
After RESTORE the next READ starts reading from the first item in the first DATA statement of the program. The optional sign is either * meaning RESTORE for numbers only, or $ meaning RESTORE for strings only.

line RETURN
Returns from a subroutine by sending control back to the statement just after the most recently executed GOSUB.

line STOP
Halts the program. The Basic system prints runtime used, then READY.

Appendix C. Commands

The Basic commands allow the user to modify programs, to run them, to move them from core to filestore and back again, and so on. All commands can be shortened to their first three letters. Command lines are terminated by Return, and acknowledged by READY when completed. They are separated from their argument(s), if any, by one or more spaces. Commands are executed immediately, if legal, not stored.

BYE	Logs the user off the system (as does GOODBYE).
COPY	COPY F1 > F2 makes a copy of the disc file F1.BAS and saves it as F2.BAS on the disc. COPY DATA>TTY: types DATA.BAS on the terminal without disturbing the working-area.
CATALOG	Lists the names of all entries on the user's file area. If followed by three asterisks as in CATALOG*** it lists the programs on the public library.
DELETE	Erases lines from the working-area. DELETE N-M erases lines N to M inclusive; DELETE I,J,K-L erases lines I, J, and K to L inclusive. Just typing a linenumber immediately followed by Return also deletes that line.
HELP	Tells the user about the more important Basic commands.
KEY	Restores control to the keyboard after a papertape has been read in using TAPE. TAPE causes suppression of the line-feed added after every carriage-return; KEY restores it. This command is terminated by Linefeed, not Return.
LIST	Lists the current contents of the working-area on the terminal preceded by its name and the time and date. LISTNH lists it with no heading. LISTREV lists it in reverse order. LIST N-M or LISTNH N-M list lines N to M with and without the heading respectively.
NEW	NEW PROG clears the working-area and establishes PROG.BAS as the current name. The user may then type in a new program. If you type in a program without giving a NEW command, it will be called NONAME.BAS. If you forget to clear out an old program before typing in a new one, the two will be mixed - probably in a confusing fashion. To rename a program without clearing core use RENAME.
OLD	Retrieves a stored program and puts it in the working-area erasing anything currently there. OLD PROG1 sets PROG1.BAS from the user's disc area and loads it into core; OLD PROG1*** loads the library program PROG1.BAS (if there is one).
QUEUE	QUEUE FNAME puts the file FNAME.BAS into the queue for output on the lineprinter.
RENAME	RENAME SMITH changes the name of the program in the working-area to SMITH.BAS.
REPLACE	REPLACE JONES finds JONES on disc, erases it, and replaces it with whatever is in the working-area under the current name.

If no file is specified, one with the current name is sought on disc for replacement.

RESEQUENCE RESEQUENCE N renumbers the lines of the working-area starting at N and increasing in steps of 10. RESEQUENCE N,,M starts at N and increments in steps of M. (Both commas are necessary.) RESEQUENCE N,I,M starts renumbering from the line currently numbered I and changes it to N, with subsequent lines incremented by M. GOTOs etc. are altered where necessary to comply with the revised numbering.

RUN Executes the program in the working-area. RUNNH suppresses the heading. RUN N starts execution at line N.

SAVE Stores the current program on disc under the current name. SAVE FNAME.EXT saves it under the name FNAME.EXT.

SCRATCH Clears the contents of the working-area, leaving it empty but not altering the current name.

TAPE Prepares for input via the papertape reader on terminals which have one. After the tape has been read in, KEY should be used to revert to normal input mode where the system automatically inserts a line-feed after every Return. To punch a program on papertape type LISNH, then turn on the tape punch, then press Return. The tape so produced can be read back later using TAPE and KEY. (To punch blank leader or trailer tape, you must switch to LOCAL and press Runout, then go back to DUPLEX.)

UNSAVE UNSAVE FNAME deletes FNAME.BAS from disc storage.

WEAVE WEAVE PROG merges PROG.BAS from disc with the current program in the working-area on a line-by-line basis. Where a statement in PROG.BAS has the same linenumber as one already in core it overwrites the one already there, otherwise the two are merged in linenumber order.

Also useful to the Basic programmer are a number of keys which have special functions, and which can be used within the Basic system. (A 'control' character prints as ^ and then the character and is obtained by holding down the CTRL key while typing the character. For instance, CTRL/C appears on the terminal as ^C.)

Return This is required to terminate all commands and input lines: the system does not accept any input (except certain special characters including those listed here) until the Return key is pressed. It causes carriage-return and line-feed.

Rubout	Pressing Rubout N times deletes the last N characters of the current input line, working backwards from the last one typed. The first Rubout causes a backslash (\) to appear followed by the character deleted. Further Rubouts cause subsequent deleted characters to appear. On resumption of normal type-in a second backslash is printed, enclosing the deleted characters (which appear in reverse order).
CTRL/C	(^C) Attracts Monitor's attention and causes return to command level. Two CTRL/Cs are needed to halt a running program unless it is awaiting input when one is sufficient.
CTRL/I	Causes a tab to the beginning of the next print zone. Zones are 8 character-positions wide.
CTRL/R	Prints the current input line without disturbing or accepting it.
CTRL/U	Erases the whole of the current input line.

You may have to experiment or consult a manual to find how to perform the equivalent operations on your system. For instance, some machines use 'Escape' for Return, 'Backspace' for Rubout, 'Break' for CTRL/C, and 'Cancel' or 'CTRL/X' for CTRL/U. This sort of (tiresome) investigation - finding your way around the system - is an essential prelude to using a new computer.

Appendix D. Basic datafile statements

The same conventions have been used in exhibiting the format of these statements as in Appendix B. In addition, where the word 'channel' appears it should be understood to represent a channel-specifier. A channel-specifier is #N, or #N: for sequential files and :N, or :N: for direct-access files, where N is any numeric formula (value 1 to 9) which will be truncated to an integer if not integral. If the statement or function which contains the channel-specifier is only applicable to sequential or to random-access files the leading # or : indicating file-type may be omitted since it is unnecessary. (Most of these statements are specific to the DEC10.)

line FILE channel string [,channel string]*

Assigns files to channels during execution, indicating file-type. The channel specifier, as explained above, may be #N, or #N: for sequential files, or :N, or :N: for random-access files, where N is a numeric formula with a value from 1 to 9. The string (any string formula) names a file and should take the form

NAME.EXT type

where type is blank for a sequential file, % for a numeric random-access file, or $N for a random-access string file (where N is an integer constant from 1 to 132 stating the maximum number of characters per record). If no record-size is specified for a string random-access file and the file does not already exist, the value 34 is assumed. If the string naming the file is a literal constant it must be in quotes.

line FILES file name [,file name]*
Assigns files to channels before program execution. Channels 1 to 9 are assigned consecutively to the files named in all FILES statements in a program during compilation. If an argument is absent (indicated by two commas with no file name between them) the channel for the missing file is skipped. Each file name is the name of a file (plus dot and extension unless it is .BAS): it is not put in quotes.

line IF END channel THEN linenumber
Sends execution to the line specified after THEN (or GOTO which may be substituted for THEN) if there is no more data to be read in the file on the specified channel.

line INPUT channel var [,var]*
Reads data from a sequential file without linenumbers or from a random-access file into the variable(s), one by one. (If used on a linenumbered file, linenumbers will be read as data.)

line MARGIN channel N [,channel N]*
Sets the right margin(s) of the output file(s) on the specified channel(s) to the position given by N which should be a numeric formula with value from 1 to 132. MARGIN only applies to sequential files since random-access files have no margin.

line MARGIN ALL numeric-formula
Sets the right margin position for all sequential files to the value of the numeric-formula, which should be from 1 to 132. It has no effect on random-access files nor on the teletype.

line NOPAGE channel [channel]*
Indicates that output to the sequential file(s) on the specified channel(s) is not to be divided into pages (normal mode), cancelling the effect of a previous PAGE statement. This statement is unnecessary unless a PAGE has been executed. It has no effect on random-access files.

line NOPAGE ALL
Sets all sequential files on channels 1 to 9 in NOPAGE mode (normal mode). It has no effect on random-access files nor on the teletype.

line NOQUOTE channel [channel]*
Puts the sequential file(s) on the specified channel(s) into NOQUOTE mode, which means that output strings are not enclosed in quotes. This is the default mode so NOQUOTE is only required after a QUOTE statement.

line NOQUOTE ALL
Places all sequential files into NOQUOTE mode. It has no effect on random-access files.

line PAGE channel N [,channel N]*
Starts dividing output to the specified sequential file(s) into pages of a given size. The numeric-formula N indicates the number of lines to a page.

line PAGE ALL numeric-formula
Sets the output page-length for all sequential files to the number of lines given by the numeric-formula.

line PRINT channel formula [separator formula]*
Prints the values of the formulas on to the file on the specified channel, according to the format dictated by the separators which can be commas, semicolons or <PA>, as in a normal PRINT statement. This statement cannot be used with linenumbered sequential files as it does not print a linenumber at the start of each line. If it is used with a random-access file, the formulas may be either string or numeric but not both, and the separators will have no effect on output format.

line PRINT channel USING image, formula [,formula]*
Outputs data to a non-linenumbered sequential file with a layout specified by the image. This can be a linenumber referring to a line beginning with a colon and containing a sequence of format-control characters, or a string containing those characters. The layout options are the same as with normal PRINT USING statements.

line QUOTE channel [channel]*
Puts the sequential file(s) on the channel(s) specified into QUOTE mode - whereby strings that contain delimiters (blanks, tabs or commas) are

output enclosed in quotes, leading blanks are inserted before strings and negative numbers, and strings may not overflow the space on one line and spill on to the next. Data written in this manner can be read back from the file into a program without being unintentionally split up.

line QUOTE ALL
Sets all sequential files to QUOTE mode; and has no effect on random-access files.

line READ channel var [,var]*
Reads data from the linenumbered sequential file on the specified channel into the variable(s), one data-item at a time. It expects every line of the file to start with a linenumber, which it ignores. It may also be used on random-access files, in which case it is equivalent to INPUT.

line RESTORE channel [channel]*
Prepares the sequential file(s) specified for reading from the first data-item, and sets the record-pointer for any random-access files specified to indicate the first record. Sequential files are in a RESTOREd state automatically at the start of a program.

line SCRATCH channel [channel]*
Erases all contents of the specified file(s) and prepares them for printing from the beginning if sequential, or resets the record-pointer to 1 if random-access.

line SET channel N [,channel N]*
Sets the record-pointer(s) for the random-access file(s) on the channel(s) specified to the value(s) of the numeric-formula(s). N is any numeric formula.

line WRITE channel formula [separator formula]*
Outputs data to the file on the specified channel, which should either be a linenumbered sequential file or a random-access file. If it is a sequential file the first line will be numbered 1000 and subsequent lines incremented by 10. If it is a random-access file this statement is equivalent to PRINT. The formating indicated by the choice of separators (commas, semicolons etc.) is irrelevant to random-access files.

line WRITE channel USING image, formula [,formula]*
Writes the value(s) of the formula(s) to a linenumbered sequential file on the specified channel, starting at line 1000 and incrementing by 10, with the output format governed by an 'image' as with the PRINT USING statement.

Note: All input and output statements (READ, WRITE, INPUT, PRINT etc.) on datafiles leave the file in a state such that the next input or output statement executed will start reading or writing where the previous one finished.

Appendix E. Matrix instructions

A special set of instructions is provided to speed and simplify computations involving matrices. In the explanations below M1, M2, M3 represent arrays; V indicates a vector; and X stands for any numeric formula. Parts in square brackets are optional.

MAT M1 = M2 All elements of M1 are given the values of the corresponding elements in M2 and the working size of M1 is reset to equal that of M2. M1 cannot be smaller than M2 and should have the same number of dimensions.

MAT M1 = M2 + M3 Adds M2 to M3 and puts the result in M1. Both M2 and M3 must be the same size. M1 may be the same matrix as M2 or M3.

MAT M1 = M2 − M3 Subtracts M3 from M3 and puts the result in M1. Conditions are the same as for matrix addition.

MAT M1 = M2 * M3 Multiplies matrix M2 by M3 giving M1. The number of columns in M2 must equal the number of rows in M3 and the same matrix may not appear on both sides of the equal sign. M1 will have the number of rows of M2 and columns of M3.

MAT M1 = (X) * M2 Multiplies each element of M2 by X to produce new values for M1. Both M1 and M2 may be the same matrix. The instruction MAT M1=(1)*M2 is one way to copy a complete array into another (of compatible size).

MAT M1 = CON [(size)] Fills matrix M1 with ones. Optionally, a new (smaller) working size may be specified by following CON with a bracketed expression. The re-dimensioning may be done with variables as well as constants. For example:
MAT A = CON(10,J).

MAT M1 = IDN [(size)] Sets M1 up as an identity matrix - all ones along the main diagonal and zeroes elsewhere. A new working size may be specified, as with CON.

MAT M1 = ZER [(size)] Fills M1 with zeroes. A new working size may be stated as with CON.

MAT M1 = INV(M2) Inverts M2 and puts it into M1. Both should be 'square' matrices with the same size. The same matrix may appear as both M1 and M2. (DET is set equal to the determinant of the matrix after inversion.)

MAT M1 = TRN(M2) Transposes M2 and puts it into M1. Matrix M1 must have as many rows as M2 has columns and vice versa. Both M1 and M2 may be the same 'square' matrix.

MAT INPUT V Calls for the input of a one-dimensional array. If the ampersand (&) is the last character on a line before Return, input continues on the next line. If there is no ampersand before Return, input is finished. The special function NUM gives the number of items entered in the latest MAT INPUT.

MAT PRINT list Prints one or more arrays. Separate arrays in the list by commas for normal spacing or by semicolons for packed output. (Matrices are printed row by row.)

MAT READ list Fills one or more arrays with data from DATA statements. New working sizes may be specified for matrices or vectors in the list, as with CON. For example: MAT READ A(N+1),B(10,I–J). (Matrices are read row by row.)

MAT instructions do not affect element zero of a vector (e.g. A(0)) or row zero (e.g. B(0,I)) or column zero (e.g. B(I,0)) of a matrix. Beginners are advised only to use the instructions for matrix addition, multiplication etc. on matrices of the same size and shape; otherwise the implicit re-dimensioning may cause problems.

The matrix features described here which are most likely to differ on other machines are MAT INPUT and the re-dimensioning capability. Check these by writing a small test program.

Appendix F. Functions

Arithmetic functions

Basic provides several predefined functions to supplement the ordinary arithmetic operations. In the explanations below X indicates any numeric formula, while N and I indicate numeric formulas that will be truncated to integers if not already integral.

ABS(X) Absolute value of X.
ATN(X) Arctangent of X where X is in radians.
COS(X) Cosine of X where X is in radians.
COT(X) Cotangent of X where X is in radians.
EXP(X) Natural exponent of X (e to the power of X).
INT(X) Truncated value of X (largest integer <= X).
LN(X) Natural logarithm of X (alternative form).
LOG(X) Natural logarithm of X (base e) where X>0.
LOG10(X) Common logarithm (base 10) of X where X>0.
RND Random number between 0 and 1.
SIN(X) Sine of X where X is in radians.
SGN(X) Returns +1 if X>0; 0 if X=0; and −1 if X<0.
SQR(X) Square-root of X where X>=0.
SQRT(X) Square-root of X (alternative form).
TAN(X) Tangent of X where X is in radians.
TIM Elapsed seconds since program began.

Matrix functions

There are also two functions for use with the MAT instructions.

DET Determinant of matrix after inversion by MAT INV.
NUM Number of items input to last MAT INPUT.

Random-access file functions

The following functions are used with random-access files. (C specifies a channel number 1 to 9 with a random-access datafile open on it.)

LOC(C) Indicates the current record on channel C.
LOF(C) Gives the last record of the file on channel C.

String functions

Finally there are a number of string functions for selecting substrings and so on.

ASC(character) Gives the ASCII code for its argument which is one character (not in quotes).

CHR$(N) Gives the character for which N is the ASCII code-number. For instance, CHR$(65)="A".

INSTR(N,string,string) Searches the first string for the second starting at the Nth character and returns the position in the first where the second one starts, if found; otherwise zero. If N, is absent 1, is assumed.

LEFT$(string,N) Returns the first N characters in the string.
LEN(string) Returns the number of characters in the string.
MID$(string,I,N) Returns the substring starting at position I in the string and containing N characters. If ,N is omitted it returns the substring from I to the end of the string.
RIGHT$(string,N) Returns the last N characters of the string.
SPACE$(N) Returns a string of N spaces.
STR$(X) Returns a string representation of the numeric value of X. Thus STR$(9.876)="9.876".
VAL(string) Gives the numerical value of the string which must look like a number, reversing STR$. Thus VAL("54.321")=54.321.

The user may also define new functions using DEF FN and use them in expressions in a program. Function definition and use is dealt with in Chapter 5. User-defined functions may take only numeric arguments and return numeric values.

Function calls may be embedded. E.g. ABS(SQR(FNJ(K*3))–8.5) is a valid function reference computing the absolute value of the difference between the square-root of FNJ(K*3) and 8.5. Since function references are one kind of arithmetic expression they may appear as arguments in another function reference.

Note: DET, NUM, LOC, LOF and most of the string functions may be implemented differently in other versions of Basic. In addition, RND and TIM may require arguments.

Appendix G. Basic computing glossary

ADP	Automatic Data Processing
ALGORITHM	Method of solving a problem in a finite number of steps
ALPHANUMERIC	Composed of letters and/or digits only
ARGUMENT	Variable passed to a SUBROUTINE or FUNCTION when it is CALLed
ARRAY	Collection of DATA under one name whose members are individually identified by SUBSCRIPTs
ARRAY-ELEMENT	Single data-item of an ARRAY
ASCII	American Standard Code for Information Interchange
BASIC	Beginner's All-purpose Symbolic Instruction Code
BINARY	Related to the number system base 2, using only the digits 0 to 1
BIT	BINARY digit - either 0 or 1

BUG	Fault in a program causing it to fail, hence 'de-bugging'
CALL	Transfer control to a SUBROUTINE
CARRIAGE-RETURN	Movement of printhead to start of line
CHAINING	Splitting a large PROGRAM into smaller linked segments
CHARACTER	Single symbol that a COMPUTER can recognize, e.g. letters (A–Z), numbers (0–9) and various other signs
CIRCULARITY	See RECURSION
COMMAND	Keyword that causes BASIC to take immediate action, such as RUN or LIST
COMPILER	Program that translates from a programming language, e.g. BASIC, into the COMPUTER's own INSTRUCTION code
COMPUTER	Machine for processing information according to a PROGRAM of instructions or Centrally Organized Method for Processing User Time Expensively and Redundantly
CONSTANT	Fixed VALUE
CORE	COMPUTER's main high-speed STORE
CPU	Central Processing Unit
DATA	Information available to a PROGRAM
DATAFILE	FILE containing DATA
DIMENSION	Range of an ARRAY SUBSCRIPT
DIRECT-ACCESS	Applied to a FILE whose RECORDs may be processed in any order
DISC-STORE	Area on magnetic disc for long-term storage of PROGRAMs and DATA
EBCDIC	Extended BINARY Coded Decimal Interchange Code
EDITING	Inserting, deleting and/or replacing lines of a PROGRAM or FILE
EOF	End of FILE
ERROR-MESSAGE	Confusing description typed by SYSTEM when something goes wrong
FILE	PROGRAM or DATA saved on disc or other backing-store
FLOATING-POINT	Notation expressing quantities as base * exponent
FLOWCHART	Diagram of the steps in a procedure or PROGRAM showing their connections

FUNCTION	Procedure yielding a result from one or more given values or ARGUMENTs
FRONT-END	COMPUTER (or multiplexor) that handles I/O for another COMPUTER
GLOBAL	Global VARIABLEs can be accessed from any part of a PROGRAM: they are not LOCAL
GLOSSARY	List of mystifying explanations not containing the word you seek
HARDWARE	The physical machinery of a COMPUTER SYSTEM
HEURISTIC	Clever method of solving a problem that will not always work but which is quicker than the corresponding ALGORITHM when it does
I/O	Short for INPUT/OUTPUT
INPUT	Getting information into the COMPUTER, also used as a verb
INSTRUCTION	PROGRAM line telling the COMPUTER what to do next
INTEGER	Whole number
JARGON	Words and phrases useful in advancing your career
LINENUMBER	Number preceding every BASIC INSTRUCTION for sequencing and EDITING
LIST	See VECTOR
LOCAL	Belonging to only one part of a PROGRAM, for instance to a FUNCTION
LOGIN	Procedure for gaining access to a TIMESHARING SYSTEM
LOGOUT	Procedure for leaving a COMPUTER SYSTEM, also known as 'logoff'
LOOP	Portion of a PROGRAM executed repeatedly
MATRIX	ARRAY of two DIMENSIONs
MONITOR	DEC10 operating-system which controls all other PROGRAMs
ON-LINE	Connected to a COMPUTER
OUTPUT	Getting results out of the COMPUTER, also used as a verb
PARAMETER	See ARGUMENT
PERIPHERAL	Device attached to a COMPUTER and used for I/O
POINTER	VARIABLE locating a RECORD in a DATAFILE, or sometimes an element in an ARRAY

PROGRAM	Sequence of COMPUTER INSTRUCTIONs
PROGRAMMER	Harmless drudge
RANDOM-ACCESS	See DIRECT-ACCESS
RECORD	Chunk of data in a RANDOM-ACCESS FILE
RECURSION	See SELF-EMBEDDING
ROUTINE	See SUBROUTINE
RUNTIME	CPU time used by a PROGRAM
SELF-EMBEDDING	See CIRCULARITY
SEQUENTIAL	Sequential FILEs can only be processed in serial order
SERIAL	See SEQUENTIAL
SOFTWARE	PROGRAMs and ROUTINEs that make the COMPUTER behave as a SYSTEM
SORT	Arrange DATA in ascending or descending order
SPECIAL-KEY	Key on TERMINAL giving a non-printing CHARACTER with a special effect (e.g. Rubout, Return etc.)
STATEMENT	See INSTRUCTION
STORE	Part of a COMPUTER where INSTRUCTIONs and DATA may be held during execution
STRING	Sequence of CHARACTERS
SUBROUTINE	Group of INSTRUCTIONs to perform a specific process
SUBSCRIPT	VALUE which locates an element in an ARRAY
SYSTEM	Vague but prestigious word
SYSTEM-LIBRARY	Collection of pre-written PROGRAMs and ROUTINEs that any user can obtain and use
TERMINAL	Keyboard device for communicating with a COMPUTER
TIMESHARING	Method of serving many users at once by one computer, by allocating short time-slices to each
VALUE	The information represented by a VARIABLE
VARIABLE	Name for a VALUE that can change during PROGRAM execution
VDU	Visual Display Unit
VECTOR	ARRAY of one DIMENSION
WORKING-AREA	Place where a BASIC PROGRAM may be run, edited or listed

Answers to selected exercises

Suggested solutions to those exercises marked by asterisks in the text are presented here. There is no uniquely right solution to any of them; but the programs here have been tested, and they work.

In each case the name of the program is displayed, and given a number. Number 2.4 refers to exercise 4 in chapter 2; number 3.8 refers to exercise 8 of chapter 3; and so on. Then the program listing is shown, followed immediately by the printout from one or more trial runs. (User input is in bold type here as in the rest of the book.)

No explanations of method are given, but the programs themselves contain plenty of REM statements and comments after the apostrophe. This should be enough to clarify their purposes to anyone who has actually attempted the problem concerned. To make them more legible, blank (numbered) lines have been inserted, as a kind of punctuation. This is allowed on the DEC10, but not in all versions of Basic. LET has not been omitted, as a point of style.

2.4 Metric

LIST

```
METRIC.ANS     14:45              17-DEC-76

1 REM** KM/MILES CONVERTER:
2 REM** 1 YARD = 0.9144 METRES.
10 PRINT "WHEN THE COMPUTER TYPES '?' "
20 PRINT "GIVE DISTANCE,UNITS"
30 PRINT "UNITS MUST BE:"
40 PRINT "0       -       STOP"
50 PRINT "1       -       KM (-> MILES)"
60 PRINT "2       -       MILES (-> KM)"
70
100 PRINT
110 INPUT D,U
120 IF U=0 THEN 900              'SIGNAL TO STOP
125 IF U=1 THEN 150
130 IF U=2 THEN 200
140 GOTO 20              'IMPROPER INPUT
145
150 REM** KM -> MILES:
160 LET K=D                      'KM
```

```
170 LET Y=K*1000/0.9144          'YARDS
175 LET M=Y/1760                 'MILES
180 GOTO 300               'PRINT SECTION
190
200 REM** MILES -> KM:
210 LET M=D                      'MILES
220 LET Y=M*1760                 'YARDS
230 LET K=Y*0.9144/1000          'KM
250
300 REM** PRINTOUT:
310 PRINT "KM","MILES"
320 PRINT K,M
330 GOTO 100               'GET NEXT INPUT
350
900 PRINT
995 PRINT "END OF METRIC<=>IMPERIAL CONVERSION
                                         PROGRAM."
999 END

READY
RUN

METRIC.ANS     14:46          17-DEC-76

WHEN THE COMPUTER TYPES '?'
GIVE DISTANCE,UNITS
UNITS MUST BE:
0        -        STOP
1        -        KM (-> MILES)
2        -        MILES (-> KM)

?1,1
KM              MILES
1               0.621371

?1,2
KM              MILES
1.60934         1

?5,5
GIVE DISTANCE,UNITS
UNITS MUST BE:
```

```
0          –        STOP
1          –        KM (–> MILES)
2          –        MILES (–> KM)

?5,1
KM                  MILES
5                   3.10686

?2,2
KM                  MILES
3.21869             2

?0,0

END OF METRIC<=>IMPERIAL CONVERSION PROGRAM.

TIME: 0.26 SECS.
```

2.8 Growth

```
LIST

GROWTH.ANS    14:49              17-DEC-76

1  REM** COMPOUND INTEREST PROGRAM:
2  REM** N.B. BETTER FORMULA IS A1=A*(1+P/100)^Y.
50  PRINT "GIVE: AMOUNT,RATE%,YEARS"
60  INPUT A,P,Y
75  LET A1=A
80  LET I=0       'YEAR COUNTER
100  LET A1=A1+(A1*P/100)
110  LET I=I+1
120  IF I<Y THEN 100
125  REM** FINISH REPETITION IF Y CYCLES PERFORMED.
150
200  PRINT
210  PRINT "AFTER ";Y;" YEARS AT ";P;" PERCENT,"
220  PRINT "INITIAL INVESTMENT OF ";A;" BECOMES ";A1
250  PRINT "(BEWARE OF INFLATION!!)"
999  END

READY
RUN

GROWTH.ANS    14:50              17-DEC-76
```

```
GIVE: AMOUNT,RATE%,YEARS
?8250,12.25,20

AFTER 20 YEARS AT 12.25 PERCENT,
INITIAL INVESTMENT OF 8250 BECOMES 83211.
(BEWARE OF INFLATION!!)

TIME: 0.10 SECS.

READY
RUN

GROWTH.ANS    14:51               17-DEC-76

GIVE: AMOUNT,RATE%,YEARS
?1,10,100

AFTER 100 YEARS AT 10 PERCENT,
INITIAL INVESTIMENT OF 1 BECOMES 13780.6
(BEWARE OF INFLATION!!)

TIME: 0.10 SECS.
```

3.4 Differ

```
LIST

DIFFER.ANS     14:53              17-DEC-76

1  REM** PROGRAM TO COMPUTE AVERAGE DEVIATION:
10  DIM X(100)
50  PRINT "HOW MANY SCORES";
55  INPUT N
60  IF N<1 THEN 999                'STOP IF NO SCORES
65  IF N<=100 THEN 100
70  PRINT "NUMBER SHOULD BE 1 TO 100, OR 0 TO HALT."
75  PRINT "PLEASE TRY AGAIN."
80  GOTO 50
95
100  PRINT "GIVE 4 SCORES PER LINE, SEPARATED BY COMMAS."
110  PRINT "(FILL OUT LAST LINE WITH ZEROES IF NECESSARY.)"
120  PRINT
125  FOR I=1 TO N BY 4
130      INPUT X(I),X(I+1),X(I+2),X(I+3)
140  NEXT I
```

```
150
200 LET S=0             'SUM
210 FOR I=1 TO N
220     LET S=S+X(I)            'ADD TO TOTAL
225 NEXT I
250 LET A=S/N           'MEAN
275 LET A1=0
300 FOR I=1 TO N
310     LET D=A-X(I)
320     IF D>0 THEN 330
325     LET D= -D       'NEGATE IF NEGATIVE
330     LET A1=A1+D     'TOTAL OF (POSITIVE) DIFFERENCES
333 NEXT I
350 LET A1=A1/N         'AVERAGE DEVIATION
360
400 PRINT
410 PRINT "NO.","SUM","MEAN","AV. DEV."
420 PRINT N,S,A,A1
430 PRINT
440 GOTO 50             'GET ANOTHER SET
999 END

READY
RUN

DIFFER.ANS    14:55         17-DEC-76

HOW MANY SCORES ?15
GIVE 4 SCORES PER LINE, SEPARATED BY COMMAS.
(FILL OUT LAST LINE WITH ZEROES IF NECESSARY.)

?98,95,89,74
?93,102,141,123
?143,116,118,103
?100,99,56,0

NO.           SUM           MEAN          AV. DEV.
15            1550          103.333       16.5778

HOW MANY SCORES ?0

TIME: 0.20 SECS
```

3.8 Series

LIST

```
SERIES.ANS      14:58              17-DEC-76

1  REM** FIBONACCI SERIES:
10  PRINT "FIBONACCI SERIES"
50  LET K=0
60  LET N1=1              'LAST
70  LET N2=0              'LAST BUT 1
75  PRINT "NUMBER","TERM"
80  PRINT 0,0             'LINE ZERO ALREADY KNOWN
90
100  LET N=N1+N2          'FORM NEXT TERM
110  LET K=K+1                      'INCREMENT COUNTER
120  PRINT K,N
125  IF N>1E5 THEN 999              'STOP IF OVER 100000
150  LET N2=N1            'REPLACE LAST BUT 1
160  LET N1=N             'REPLACE LAST
175  GOTO 100
999  END
```

```
READY
```

RUN

```
SERIES.ANS      14:59              17-DEC-76

FIBONACCI SERIES
NUMBER          TERM
0               0
1               1
2               2
3               3
4               5
5               8
6               13
7               21
8               34
9               55
10              89
11              144
12              233
```

```
13          377
14          610
15          987
16          1597
17          2584
18          4181
19          6765
20          10946
21          17711
22          28657
23          46368
24          75025
25          121393

TIME: 0.22 SECS.
```

4.3 Invest

LIST

```
INVEST.ANS    15:01          17-DEC-76

1 REM** CALCULATES INTEREST TABLE:
10 DIM A(12)
50 PRINT "WHAT IS INITIAL AMOUNT (1 TO 5000)";
55 INPUT A
60 IF A<1 THEN 80
65 IF A<=5000 THEN 100
70 PRINT "TOO LARGE!"
75 GOTO 50
80 PRINT "TOO SMALL!"
85 GOTO 50
90
100 FOR I=2 TO 12 BY 2
101     LET A(I)=A        'SET INITIAL VALUES
105 NEXT I
110 PRINT "COMPOUND INTEREST TABLE, INITIAL AMOUNT = ";A
120 PRINT
125 PRINT "PERIOD";
130 FOR I=2 TO 12 BY 2
133     PRINT TAB(5*I-2);I;"%";
135 NEXT I
```

```
140 PRINT
144 FOR P=1 TO 25
150     FOR I=2 TO 12 BY 2
160         LET A(I)=A(I)+(A(I)*I/100)
170     NEXT I
175     PRINT USING 177, P,A(2),A(4),A(6),A(8),A(10),A(12)
177     :## #####.## #####.## #####.## #####.##
                                  #####.## #####.##
180 NEXT P
999 END

READY
RUN

INVEST.ANS      15:02              17-DEC-76

WHAT IS INITIAL AMOUNT (1 TO 5000) ?1000
COMPOUND INTEREST TABLE, INITIAL AMOUNT = 1000
```

PERIOD	2%	4%	6%	8%	10%	12%
1	1020.00	1040.00	1060.00	1080.00	1100.00	1120.00
2	1040.40	1081.60	1123.60	1166.40	1210.00	1254.40
3	1061.21	1124.86	1191.02	1259.71	1331.00	1404.93
4	1082.43	1169.86	1262.48	1360.49	1464.10	1573.52
5	1104.08	1216.65	1338.23	1469.33	1610.51	1762.34
6	1126.16	1265.32	1418.12	1586.87	1771.56	1973.82
7	1148.69	1315.93	1503.63	1713.82	1948.72	2210.68
8	1171.66	1368.57	1593.85	1850.93	2143.59	2475.96
9	1195.09	1423.31	1689.48	1999.00	2357.95	2773.08
10	1218.99	1480.24	1790.85	2158.93	2593.74	3105.85
11	1243.37	1539.45	1898.30	2331.64	2853.12	3478.55
12	1268.24	1601.03	2012.20	2518.17	3138.43	3895.98
13	1293.61	1665.07	2132.93	2719.62	3452.27	4363.49
14	1319.48	1731.68	2260.90	2937.19	3797.50	4887.11
15	1345.87	1800.94	2396.56	3172.17	4177.25	5473.57
16	1372.79	1872.98	2540.35	3425.94	4594.97	6130.39
17	1400.24	1947.90	2692.77	3700.02	5054.47	6866.04
18	1428.25	2025.82	2854.34	3996.02	5559.92	7689.97
19	1456.81	2106.85	3025.60	4315.70	6115.91	8612.76
20	1485.95	2191.12	3207.14	4660.96	6727.50	9646.29
21	1515.67	2278.77	3399.56	5033.83	7400.25	10803.85
22	1545.98	2369.92	3603.54	5436.54	8140.28	12100.31

PERIOD	2%	4%	6%	8%	10%	12%
23	1576.90	2464.72	3819.75	5871.46	8954.30	13552.35
24	1608.44	2563.30	4048.93	6341.18	9849.73	15178.63
25	1640.61	2665.84	4291.87	6848.48	10834.71	17000.06

TIME: 0.82 SECS.

4.5 Histog

LIST

```
HISTOG.ANS     15:06               17-DEC-76

1 REM** PRODUCES HISTOGRAM (SIDEWAYS):
10 DIM X(100)
20 REM** READ NUMBER OF SCORES:
25 READ N
30 IF N<1 THEN 50
35 IF N>100 THEN 50
40 GOTO 100
50 PRINT "ONLY 1 TO 100 SCORES PLEASE."
60 PRINT "RE-EXAMINE DATA STATEMENTS."
70 STOP
90
100 REM** FIND MAX FOR SCALING:
110 F9=0              'MAX. FREQUENCY
120 FOR I=1 TO N      'READ AND CHECK FREQUENCIES
122     READ F
125     IF F<0 THEN 150
130     IF F>999999 THEN 150
140     GOTO 200
150     REM** DATA ERROR:
155     PRINT "ERROR IN DATA ITEM ";I
160     PRINT "FREQUENCY OF ";F;" IS OUT OF BOUNDS
                                          (0—999999)"
166     STOP
200     IF F>F9 THEN 250
225     GOTO 270
250     LET F9=F          'NEW MAX.
270     LET X(I)=F
275 NEXT I
290
```

```
300 REM** SCALING FOR WIDTH:
303 LET F1=0
320 PRINT
330 PRINT "SCALED FROM 0 TO ";F9
333 PRINT "1 STAR = ";F9/66;" UNITS. "
340 PRINT
350 FOR I=1 TO N
355     LET T=X(I)/F9
360     PRINT I;TAB(4);"!";
365     FOR J=0 TO (T*66-0.5)
370         PRINT "*";
375     NEXT J
380     PRINT
385 NEXT I
390
500 DATA 24
501 DATA 41,29,36
502 DATA 30,27,33
503 DATA 29,21,23
504 DATA 24,20,20
505 DATA 25,11,15
506 DATA 14,12,10
507 DATA 18,10,11
508 DATA 17,08,10
999 END

READY
RUN

HISTOG.ANS     15:08          17-DEC-76

SCALED FROM 0 TO 41
1 STAR = 0.621212 UNITS.

1   !******************************************************************
2   !***********************************************
3   !**********************************************************
4   !************************************************
5   !*******************************************
6   !*****************************************************
7   !***********************************************
8   !**********************************
```

```
9   !*************************************
10  !***************************************
11  !********************************
12  !********************************
13  !*****************************************
14  !******************
15  !************************
16  !***********************
17  !*******************
18  !****************
19  !*****************************
20  !****************
21  !******************
22  !***************************
23  !*************
24  !****************
TIME: 0.66 SECS.
```

5.4 Gamble

LIST

```
GAMBLE.ANS    15:11                17-DEC-76

1  REM* TEST OF DICE-FUNCTION:
10  DIM N(6)
20  DEF FND=INT(RND*6)+1
25  REM* THIS SIMULATES A DICE-THROW (1 TO 6).
30  PRINT "THE DIE IS CAST . . ."
50  RANDOMIZE
60  MAT N=ZER                'SET N(1–6) TO ZERO
100  REM* TRY IT 600 TIMES:
110  FOR K=1 TO 600
120      LET X=FND        'THROW IT
122      LET N(X)=N(X)+1             'INCREMENT FREQUENCY
125  NEXT K
130
140  REM* OUTPUT:
150  PRINT
160  PRINT "FACE","FREQUENCY"
```

```
170 FOR K=1 TO 6
175     PRINT K,N(K)
180 NEXT K
185 PRINT
190 PRINT "EACH FACE SHOULD COME UP ABOUT 100 TIMES:"
200 PRINT "ARE THE DICE LOADED??"
999 END
```

READY
RUN

```
GAMBLE.ANS    15:12              17-DEC-76

THE DIE IS CAST . . .

FACE            FREQUENCY
1               90
2               101
3               117
4               105
5               108
6               79

EACH FACE SHOULD COME UP ABOUT 100 TIMES:
ARE THE DICE LOADED??

TIME: 0.52 SECS.

READY
```

5.6 Taxman

LIST

```
TAXMAN.ANS    15:14              17-DEC-76

1  REM** TEST OF TAXING FUNCTION:
10 DEF FNT(P)
20 LET FNT=0
25 IF P<875 THEN 99              'NO TAX TO PAY
30 IF P>5000 THEN 60
40 LET FNT=0.35*(P-875)          'STANDARD RATE
```

```
50  GOTO 99                          'EXIT
60  LET FNT=0.35*4125 + (P—5000)/2
99  FNEND
100
110  PRINT "ANNUAL INCOME";
115  INPUT I
120  IF I<0 THEN 900                 'STOP
122  LET T=FNT(I)                    'COMPUTE TAX DUE
125  PRINT
150  PRINT "GROSS","TAX","NET"
170  PRINT I,T,I—T
175  PRINT
180  GOTO 110
800
900  PRINT "YOU ARE BANKRUPT!"
909  PRINT "THE TAXMAN IS NO LONGER INTERESTED."
999  END

READY
RUN

TAXMAN.ANS    15:15              17-DEC-76

ANNUAL INCOME ?885

GROSS          TAX               NET
885            3.5               881.5

ANNUAL INCOME ?50000

GROSS          TAX               NET
50000          23943.8           26056.3

ANNUAL INCOME ?500000

GROSS          TAX               NET
500000         248944            251056

ANNUAL INCOME ?—1
YOU ARE BANKRUPT!
THE TAXMAN IS NO LONGER INTERESTED.

TIME: 0.34 SECS.
```

6.6 Merger

LIST

```
MERGER.ANS    15:16                17-DEC-76

1  REM** PROGRAM TO MERGE 2 (SORTED) STRING VECTORS:
10  DIM A$(100),B$(100),C$(200)
20  REM** INFORMATION GIVEN IN DATA STATEMENTS FROM
                                                  LINE 800.
50  READ A9,B9              'NUMBER OF STRINGS IN EACH VECTOR
55  REM** TEST FOR BAD DATA:
60  IF A9>100 THEN 90
70  IF A9<0 THEN 90
75  IF B9>100 THEN 90
80  IF B9<0 THEN 90
85  GOTO 100                'SIZE LIMITS OK
90  PRINT A9;" AND ";B9;" SHOULD BOTH LIE BETWEEN 1 & 100!"
95  PRINT "RE-TYPE DATA STATEMENTS."
96  STOP
100  REM** READ IN THE STRINGS FOR A$ & B$:
101  LET A$(0)=B$(0)=" " 'DUMMY ELEMENT 0
110  FOR A=1 TO A9
120      READ A$(A)
122      IF A$(A-1)>A$(A) THEN 200       'OUT OF ORDER
125  NEXT A
150  FOR B=1 TO B9
160      READ B$(B)
166      IF B$(B-1)>B$(B) THEN 200       'OUT OF ORDER
170  NEXT B
180  GOTO 250
200  REM** STRINGS NOT IN ORDER:
210  PRINT "STRINGS MUST BE IN ASCENDING ORDER!"
220  GOTO 95
225
250  REM** NOW MERGE THEM:
255  LET N=A=B=1         'INITIALIZE COUNTERS
300  IF A>A9 THEN 500            'A$ IS EXHAUSTED
310  IF B>B9 THEN 550            'B$ EMPTY
320  IF A$(A)>B$(B) THEN 400
330  IF A$(A)<B$(B) THEN 440
333  REM** GETS HERE IF BOTH STRINGS THE SAME.
```

```
350  LET B=B+1
355  GOSUB 1000
360  REM** DOES NOT DUPLICATE IDENTICAL ENTRIES.
365  GOTO 300                'NEXT COMPARISON
400  REM** B$ ENTRY IS SMALLER
410  GOSUB 1050              'ADD B$(B) TO C$
420  GOTO 300
440  REM** A$ ENTRY IS SMALLER
450  GOSUB 1000              'ADD A$(A) TO C$
460  GOTO 300
475
500  REM** A$ EMPTY, FINISH OFF B$
505  IF B>B9 THEN 600                  'ALL DONE
510  GOSUB 1050              'ADD B$ ENTRY
520  GOTO 505
550  REM** B$ EMPTY, FINISH A$
555  IF A>A9 THEN 600                  'ALL DONE
560  GOSUB 1000              'ADD A$ ENTRY
570  GOTO 555                'REPEAT TILL ALL A$ COPIED
575
600  PRINT
610  FOR I=1 TO N
620  PRINT C$(I)
625  NEXT I
666  STOP
700
775  REM** TEST DATA:
800  DATA 4,8
801  DATA ADAM,EVE,GOD,SATAN
802  DATA  ABEL,ADAM,APPLE,CAIN,EDEN,EVE,GOD,SERPENT
1000  REM** ROUTINE TO ADD TO C$:
1001  REM** HAS 2 ENTRY POINTS.
1010  LET C$(N)=A$(A)              '1ST ENTRY POINT (USE A$)
1020  LET A=A+1                    'INCREMENT A$ INDEX
1030  GOTO 1090                    'EXIT
1050  LET C$(N)=B$(B)              '2ND ENTRY POINT (USE B$)
1060  LET B=B+1                    'INCREMENT B$ INDEX
1090  LET N=N+1                    'INCREMENT C$ INDEX
1099  RETURN
9999  END
```

```
READY
RUN

MERGER.ANS    15:20                 17-DEC-76

ABEL
ADAM
APPLE
CAIN
EDEN
EVE
GOD
SATAN
SERPENT

TIME: 0.22 SECS.
```

6.9 Backwd

```
LIST

BACKWD.ANS    15:21                 17-DEC-76

1  REM** TEST OF STRING-REVERSING SUBROUTINES:
50  PRINT "INPUT STRING:"
60  INPUT A$               'TEST STRING
90
100  REM** MODE (M) IS 1 OR 2:
101  FOR M=1 TO 2
110      LET T0=TIM        'USE BUILT-IN TIMING FUNCTION
120      FOR N=1 TO 1000            'TRY 1000 REPS
125         LET X$=A$     'INPUT STRING
130         ON M GOTO 140,160   '2-WAY FORK
140         GOSUB 1000   '1ST METHOD
150         GOTO 175
160         GOSUB 2000   '2ND METHOD
170         GOTO 175
175      NEXT N
180      REM** LINE 170 JUST TO KEEP OVERHEAD EQUAL.
190
200      LET T1=TIM        'GET NEW RUNTIME VALUE
210      PRINT
```

```
220     PRINT "METHOD ";M
222     PRINT "TOOK";T1-T0;"SECONDS OF RUN-TIME"
225     PRINT "TO CONVERT"
230     PRINT TAB(4);A$
240     PRINT "INTO"
250     PRINT TAB(4);X$
255     PRINT "1000 TIMES."
260     PRINT
300 NEXT M
333 STOP
1000 REM** STRING REVERSAL ROUTINE, USING 'CHANGE':
1001 REM** X$ IS REVERSED; I,J,L ALSO USED.
1010 DIM X(100),Y(100)              'WORK VECTORS
1020 LET L=LEN(X$)
1025 IF L<=100 THEN 1040                    'TOO LONG?
1030 GOTO 1500           'ERROR SECTION
1040 CHANGE X$ TO X
1050 FOR I=1 TO L
1060     LET J=L-I+1                'COUNT BACKWARDS IN J
1070     LET Y(J)=X(I)
1075 NEXT I
1080 LET Y(0)=L                     'PUT LENGTH IN ZERO LOCATION
1090 CHANGE Y TO X$
1099 RETURN              'WITH RESULT IN X$
1200
1500 REM** ERROR IN STRING LENGTH:
1505 PRINT "STRING: ";X$
1510 PRINT "IS WRONG SIZE!"
1515 STOP
1600
2000 REM** STRING REVERSAL ROUTINE, USING
                                    CONCATENATION:
2001 REM** X$ IS REVERSED; L,Y$ ALSO USED.
2005 LET L=LEN(X$)
2010 IF L<=100 THEN 2020
2015 GOTO 1500       'ERROR IN LENGTH
2020 IF L<1 THEN 2015               'TOO SHORT
2022 LET Y$=""           'START WITH NULL STRING
2025 LET Y$=Y$+MID$(X$,L,1)                 '1 CH FROM POSITION L
2030 LET L=L-1           'REDUCE L
```

```
2050 IF L>0 THEN 2025            'REPEAT TILL L=0
2060 LET X$=Y$
2080 RETURN             'WITH RESULT IN X$
2500
3000 REM** METHOD 2 TAKES LONGER;
3003 REM** BUT METHOD 1 REQUIRES MORE SPACE, FOR WORK
                                                    VECTORS.
9999 END

READY
RUN

BACKWD.ANS    15:24            17-DEC-76

INPUT STRING:
?THE 1ST SHALL BE LAST & THE LAST SHALL BE 1ST.

METHOD 1
TOOK 13.04 SECONDS OF RUN-TIME
TO CONVERT
  THE 1ST SHALL BE LAST & THE LAST SHALL BE 1ST.
INTO
  .TS1 EB LLAHS TSAL EHT & TSAL EB LLAHS TS1 EHT
1000 TIMES.

METHOD 2
TOOK 56.26 SECONDS OF RUN-TIME
TO CONVERT
  THE 1ST SHALL BE LAST & THE LAST SHALL BE 1ST.
INTO
  .TS1 EB LLAHS TSAL EHT & TSAL EB LLAHS TS1 EHT
1000 TIMES.

TIME: 69.54 SECS.
```

7.6 Length

```
LIST

LENGTH.ANS    15:33            17-DEC-76

1  REM** COUNTS NUMBER OF WORDS PER SENTENCE ON FILE#1:
10  FILES HAMLET.SEQ
20  REM** CHANGE LINE 10 TO READ DIFFERENT FILE
                                    (IN SAME FORMAT).
```

```
25  DIM F(100)
30
50  REM** INITIALIZE:
60  RESTORE#1
70  LET W=T=S=0
90
100  IF END#1 THEN 500           'PRINT RESULTS IF FILE ALL READ
110  READ#1, W$            'GET ONE STRING
120  IF W$="." THEN 200
125  IF W$="?" THEN 200
130  IF W$="!" THEN 200
140  IF W$=";" THEN 100           'IGNORE SEMICOLON
145  IF W$=":" THEN 100           'IGNORE COLON
150  LET W=W+1             '1 MORE WORD
160  GOTO 100              'REPEAT
175
200  REM** END OF SENTENCE:
210  LET T=T+W             'TOTAL OF WORDS
220  LET S=S+1             'NUMBER OF SENTENCES
225  LET F(W)=F(W)+1              'FREQUENCY COUNT
230  LET W=0               'RESET WORDS IN CURRENT SENTENCE
250  GOTO 100              'START NEW SENTENCE
400
500  REM** RESULTS:
505  PRINT
510  PRINT "TOTAL","TOTAL","AVERAGE"
515  PRINT "WORDS","SENTENCES","WORDS PER SENTENCE"
520  PRINT T,S,T/S
525  PRINT
550  PRINT "FREQUENCY DISTRIBUTION:"
555  PRINT "NO. OF WORDS","FREQUENCY"
560  FOR I=1 TO 100
570  IF F(I)<1 THEN 580
575  PRINT I,F(I)
580  NEXT I
600
999  END

READY
RUN
```

```
LENGTH.ANS    15:35          17-DEC-76

TOTAL         TOTAL          AVERAGE
WORDS         SENTENCES      WORDS PER SENTENCE
262           21             12.4762

FREQUENCY DISTRIBUTION:
NO. OF WORDS             FREQUENCY
2                        2
3                        2
4                        1
5                        3
6                        2
9                        1
10                       1
12                       1
13                       1
17                       1
21                       1
24                       1
27                       1
28                       1
29                       1
31                       1

TIME: 1.02 SECS.
```

7.7 Binary

```
LIST

BINARY.ANS    15:37          17-DEC-76

1 REM** BINARY SEARCH OF SORTED NUMERIC RAX FILE:
10 FILES DATA.RAX%
20 RESTORE:1
50 LET U=LOF(1)           'UPPER BOUND IS LAST RECORD
55 LET L=1                'LOWER BOUND STARTS AT 1
60 REM** ITEM SOUGHT MUST LIE BETWEEN L AND U
100 REM** GET SOUGHT KEY VALUE:
110 PRINT "GIVE SEARCH KEY";
120 INPUT K
150
```

```
155 PRINT "SEARCH HISTORY:"
160 PRINT "LOWER","UPPER","MIDPT.","VALUE"
200 REM** LOOK ON FILE FOR VALUE K:
210 IF L>=U THAN 500             'EXIT, FAILURE
220 LET M=INT((U-L)/2)           'CALCULATE MIDPOINT OF
                                           POSSIBLE RANGE
222 LET M=L+M                    'OFFSET BY LOWER BOUND
225 SET :1,M                     'SET FILE POINTER TO RECORD M
250 READ:1, X                    'READ VALUE AT RECORD M
255 PRINT L,U,M,X                'PRINT TRACE-OUT VALUES
275 IF X=K THEN 400              'EXIT, SUCCESS
280 IF X<K THEN 300              'TOO LOW
285 REM** GETS HERE IF X>K:
290 LET U=M                      'RESET UPPER BOUND
295 GOTO 200                     'REPEAT IN REDUCED SEARCH-
                                                   AREA
300 REM** X WAS TOO SMALL:
310 LET L=M+1
315 REM** RESET LOWER BOUND (+1 TO COUNTERACT
                                     TRUNCATION).
320 GOTO 200              'REPEAT IN REDUCED SEARCH-AREA
330
400 REM** K WAS FOUND:
410 PRINT
420 PRINT "KEY ";X;" FOUND AT LOCATION ";M
425 STOP
500 REM** K NOT FOUND:
505 PRINT
510 PRINT "KEY ";K;" NOT FOUND."
555 END

READY
RUN

BINARY.ANS    15:39          17-DEC-76

GIVE SEARCH KEY ?45
SEARCH HISTORY:
LOWER         UPPER          MIDPT.          VALUE
1             40             20              50
1             20             10              25
11            20             15              35
```

```
LOWER          UPPER          MIDPT.         VALUE
16             20             18             44
19             20             19             48

KEY 45 NOT FOUND.

TIME: 0.30 SECS.

READY
RUN

BINARY.ANS     15:40          17-DEC-76

GIVE SEARCH KEY ?44
SEARCH HISTORY:
LOWER          UPPER          MIDPT.         VALUE
1              40             20             50
1              20             10             25
11             20             15             35
16             20             18             44

KEY 44 FOUND AT LOCATION 18

TIME: 0.24 SECS.
```

Index